"At the Reformation's five hundredth anniversary, Erwin Lutzer reminds us not only why the Reformation is one of the most significant events in Western history but also why it still holds important lessons for the church today. As Lutzer demonstrates in this book, the theological convictions of Luther, Zwingli, and Calvin need to be recovered as an antidote to the watered-down gospel proclaimed from many Protestant pulpits in our day. Every Protestant needs to recognize the incredible theological debt we owe to the Reformers. Let this book introduce you to their lives, their ministries, and, most importantly, their theology."

R. Albert Mohler Jr., president of the Southern Baptist
Theological Seminary

"If we truly want to be relevant today, we must proclaim the ancient gospel. The gospel that Jesus and the apostles proclaimed in the first century is the gospel that Martin Luther and the Reformers proclaimed in the sixteenth century, and it is the same gospel we must proclaim today. With pastoral wisdom and passion, Dr. Lutzer explores the remarkable story of the Reformation, and he powerfully demonstrates why the story of the Reformation is, in fact, our story. Dr. Lutzer sounds a much-needed clarion call to a generation that is quickly turning away from the one and only gospel. I am grateful to our God that Dr. Lutzer has provided us with a refreshingly enjoyable and accessible look at the Reformation and what the Reformation was all about—the unchanging gospel of Jesus Christ."

Burk Parsons, copastor of Saint Andrew's Chapel;
editor of *Tabletalk* magazine

"Those who do not learn from history are doomed to repeat it. *Rescuing the Gospel* is a wonderful journey through the history of the pre-Reformation and Reformation periods that will illumine what people need to know about the gospel, God's grace, the church, and religious liberty. These are crucial topics for our day, when so many opinions about them exist. As the book shows, history has much to teach us here. Erwin Lutzer's study shows us in a most informative and interesting way what we should learn from this crucial period of our past history."

Darrell Bock, executive director for cultural engagement
at the Howard G. Hendricks Center for Christian Leadership
and Cultural Engagement; senior research professor
of New Testament studies at Dallas Theological Seminary

"Many books will be written about the five hundredth anniversary of the Reformation. But few, if any, will be written with such spiritual sensitivity, theological depth, or historical accuracy as Erwin Lutzer's *Rescuing the Gospel*. Capturing the pageantry and danger following Martin Luther's bold stand in Wittenberg, Lutzer has penned what may be his most important book—a book that looks back on the glories of the original Reformation and looks forward to the hope of a new reformation."

Robert Jeffress, senior pastor of First Baptist Church Dallas; author of *Not All Roads Lead to Heaven*

"The fastest way to kill a tree is to cut its roots! And Dr. Erwin Lutzer helps prevent us from doing that. We must never forget our spiritual and historical root system. We build upon the shoulders of those who have labored in the past. *Rescuing the Gospel* will introduce (or reintroduce) you to some forebears of our faith who fought hard to make the Scriptures the central for authority and practice. I have enjoyed every book Erwin Lutzer has written. He makes me think and helps me learn. In *Rescuing the Gospel* he does even more. He rekindles a love for the truth and helps us understand and appreciate the enormous contribution of the great Reformers to the roots of the gospel tree."

Skip Heitzig, senior pastor of Calvary Albuquerque

"A powerful evidence for the continuing importance of Luther's Reformation is seen when one of the most influential evangelical pastors of our day writes a solid theological book in its favor. Dr. Erwin Lutzer, pastor emeritus of Moody Church in Chicago, has done just that—and every evangelical would benefit greatly from reading it. Particularly important is the author's recognition that the differences between Catholics and Protestants on the central doctrine of justification have *not* been transcended but remain an obstacle to the unity of the church militant."

John Warwick Montgomery, professor emeritus of law and humanities at the University of Bedfordshire, England; distinguished research professor of philosophy at Concordia University Wisconsin; director of the International Academy of Apologetics, Evangelism & Human Rights, Strasbourg, France

"A distance of five centuries can dull our appreciation for the revolutionizing impact of the Reformation. I deeply appreciate the clarity and candor of *Rescuing the Gospel*. It is only as we refresh our minds with the theological and historical realities of what was spawned by the courage of Wycliffe, Hus, Luther, and others that we can discern right paths in our day. The proclamation of the pure gospel message is still urgently needed today. This book calls, corrects, and challenges us to that end."

Paul Nyquist, president of Moody Bible Institute

"Hus, Wycliffe, Luther, the Reformation, freedom, faith—these people and these words have their theological/biblical roots in 'grace alone, faith alone, in Christ alone,' the enduring emphases of the Reformation. Dr. Erwin Lutzer, pastor emeritus of Moody Church in Chicago, delivers a well-researched work that shows the Reformation not as an ivory tower discussion of dispassionate theologians but as a dynamic movement of people, pastoral leaders, and lay leaders whose concern was for the forgiveness, life, and salvation that come to people as a gift of God's grace. Squarely positioned in the evangelical tradition, Dr. Lutzer gives all people of every religious stripe something to think deeply about when speaking of Christ and His grace for their lives today. As you read this book, you will realize anew why these discussions mattered five hundred years ago and why they still matter today."

Gregory Seltz, speaker on *The Lutheran Hour*;
previously professor of theology
at Concordia University Irvine

"Erwin Lutzer helpfully traces the basic events and teachings of the Reformers in a fashion that readers can easily understand. This little Reformation 101 book reminds us that the Reformation still matters— and why. Reading this book will whet your appetite for more information about the Reformation and its powerful, biblical teachings."

Joel R. Beeke, president of Puritan Reformed
Theological Seminary

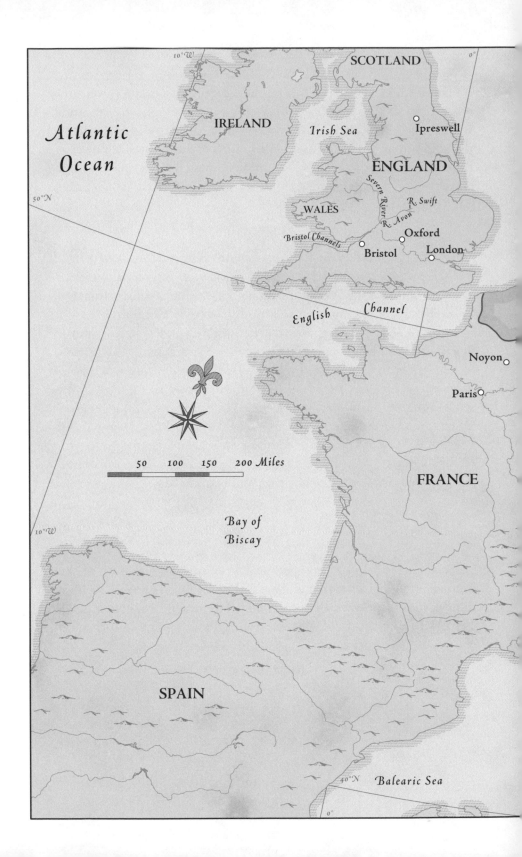

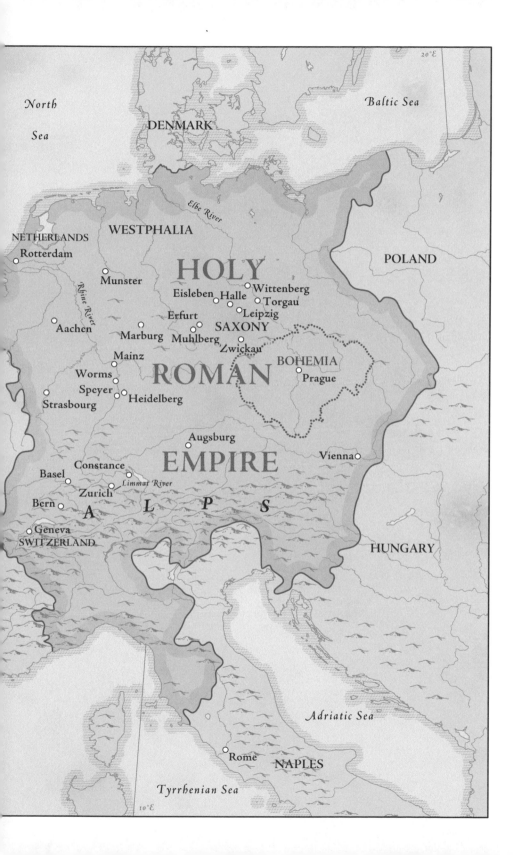

RESCUING THE GOSPEL

The Story and Significance of the Reformation

ERWIN W. LUTZER

BakerBooks

a division of Baker Publishing Group
Grand Rapids, Michigan

© 2016 by Erwin Lutzer

Published by Baker Books
a division of Baker Publishing Group
P.O. Box 6287, Grand Rapids, MI 49516-6287
www.bakerbooks.com

Printed in the United States of America

Library of Congress Cataloging-in-Publication Data
Names: Lutzer, Erwin W., author.
Title: Rescuing the Gospel : the story and significance of the Reformation / Erwin W. Lutzer.
Description: Grand Rapids, MI : Baker Books, 2016. | Includes bibliographical references.
Identifiers: LCCN 2015040636 (print) | LCCN 2015042411 (ebook) | ISBN 9780801017131 (cloth) | ISBN 9781493401604 (ebook)
Subjects: LCSH: Reformation.
Classification: LCC BR305.3 .L89 2016 (print) | LCC BR305.3 (ebook) | DDC 270.6—dc23

LC record available at http://lccn.loc.gov/2015040636

Interior design by Brian Brunsting

16 17 18 19 20 21 22   7 6 5 4 3 2 1

To John Ankerberg—
defender of the faith,
lover of the gospel,
faithful friend.

I thank God that He has appointed you to His service
so that you might "contend for the faith that was once
for all delivered to the saints" (Jude 1:3).

Contents

Acknowledgments

Thanks to Brian Vos, who came to Chicago and explained his vision for this book and why he thought I should write it! My thanks also to James Korsmo, along with the entire team at Baker Books.

There have been many dozens of books written about Luther, but I am grateful for the classic *Here I Stand* by Roland Bainton and *Luther: Man between God and the Devil* by Heiko A. Oberman. I have quoted from these writers extensively and am thankful for their scholarship and insights.

Finally, I pay special tribute to my lovely wife, Rebecca, who knows only too well that when her husband has a book to write, he spends an inordinate amount of time at his computer. Without her patience and encouragement this book would never have been written. Thanks, also, Rebecca, for your help and companionship in the many trips we have taken to see the Luther sites in Germany! I look forward to us having the privilege of introducing more people to the Reformation.

Introduction

Join Me on a Journey

Thank you for joining me on this important journey.

We'll visit Wittenberg, Worms, Erfurt, Geneva, and Zurich. We'll walk through cathedrals, listen to a sermon in a town square, and meet some people whose intellect and courage shook the world. We'll listen to a story of courage and cowardice, of betrayal and faith. And when we are finished, we'll understand ourselves—and our society—much better. Best of all, new appreciation for the one message that can actually change the world will burn within us.

Someone has said that for many Christians, church history began with the first Billy Graham crusade. They think that as long as we derive our beliefs from the Bible, we can ignore the two-thousand-year history of God's people. Church history, they reason, is really only of benefit to scholars and historians. What possible relevance could the past have for the present?

How easy it is to forget that we are heirs of a rich history that began with the New Testament and continues on to this present day. To study church history is to study the ways of God; it is to appreciate His providential guidance of His people. We forget that *the better we understand yesterday, the better we will understand today.*

"The Reformation" refers to a spiritual rebirth that took place in Europe back in the sixteenth century. Many of us believe that it is, by all accounts, the most important recovery of the gospel since the days of the New Testament. When the Reformers were forced to define their faith in the crucible of controversy and hot debate, their conclusions had ramifications that shook their world—and we can still feel their influence. Look around the evangelical world today and you'll agree that we have to rediscover these same truths if we want our own churches to be all they can be for the glory of God.

Many people ignore the fundamental beliefs of the Reformation, thinking that there might be a better way to rescue our nation from the assault of secularism, pagan spirituality, and the proliferation of false religions. Others are unaware of what the fundamental issues of the Reformation really were, much less appreciate their relevance for today's world. The doctrinal apathy among many Christians in our nation is deserving of tears.

Church growth experts tell us that most people seeking a new church care little about its doctrine. They're mostly interested in the facilities of the church, its nursery, and opportunities for friendship. In fact, we are told that doctrinal teaching in new members' classes will actually turn people away rather than encourage them to join the church. The experts tell us that today's church members will switch churches at a moment's notice if they think that their personal and relational needs will be better met elsewhere—even if the doctrine taught is, at best, suspect. Thus some will opt for better facilities and architecture even at the expense of jeopardizing their own soul.

As long as indulgences are no longer for sale in a town square, and as long as the pope is no longer squandering the coffers of the church to finance unrestrained sensuality, then, as many believe, the issues of

The main image depicts Martin Luther burning the papal bull of excommunication. Episodes from the life of Luther and portraits of other Reformers make up the border.

the Reformation are no longer relevant. How wrong! Nearly all of the conflicts of the Reformation are still ongoing today, albeit with different players and in a different context. Woody Allen was right: "History repeats itself. It has to—nobody listens the first time around."[1]

I'm glad you think differently. The fact that you've read this far tells me that you are interested in the past because you know that it will shed light on the present. You're willing to join our journey and learn more about the truths that made the church great. You will be rewarded; I promise.

On our journey we're going to work through several topics.

We'll begin by examining Martin Luther's own spiritual journey and pinpoint the most important questions we need to ask ourselves about theology: How can a sinner stand in the presence of God? How perfect do we have to be in order to get to heaven? We'll sketch just enough of the background so that you'll see the conflict between Protestant and Catholic doctrine in context. And in the process, you might discover that the gospel you've heard falls short of its full, robust biblical implications.

Along the way, we'll ask (and answer) the following questions:

Do only good people go to heaven? If so, how good do we have to be?

Do priests and pastors have special privileges in the sight of God that are not accessible to ordinary believers?

What is the nature of the church? Should we have a regional church that encompasses all who live in a geographical area, or should it be limited to those who have personally trusted in Christ?

To what extent should we accept tradition into our church life and belief system? Is all tradition bad? If not, what should we keep, and what should we discard?

What does it mean to say that Christ is "the head of the church"? And how does your answer impact whatever church you happen to attend?

When you participate in the Lord's Supper, are you literally or symbolically eating and drinking Christ's body and blood? And is infant baptism the means of entry into the Christian life?

And perhaps most important, we will answer the question, "Is the Reformation over?"

At the root of these matters is the issue of *sola Scriptura*, that is, whether the Bible is sufficient and complete as a revelation from God. We will discover that in Luther's time, as in ours, there were many who denied that the Bible is the sole basis for faith and practice. Today, we are awash with self-styled prophets and preachers who claim to receive additional revelations directly from God. Luther was outraged at the claims made by such prophets in his day, and many of our televangelists would do well to listen to what he had to say.

We'll also consider the matter of freedom of religion. We who live in the West take freedom of religion for granted without realizing that throughout most of the church's two-thousand-year history there were no such freedoms. Heretics—often sincere Christians—were burned at the stake. When Luther gave his famous pronouncement at the Diet of Worms, "My conscience is taken captive by the Word of God. . . . To go against conscience is neither right nor safe," he was opposing more than a thousand years of church tradition. Indeed, he was the one who planted the seeds of freedom of conscience that were realized in the Peace of Westphalia in 1648. We dare not take this precious gift for granted.

Ulrich Zwingli pastored the Grossmünster (Great Cathedral) in Zurich.

The Reformation also speaks to our own day about the relationship between the church and the state. Although "separation of church and state" is an idea largely attributed to the United States, the Reformers tackled the topic and often differed as to how Christians should relate to civil authorities. Luther believed that the state (civil authorities) should correct the abuses of a corrupt church. Yet he strongly opposed Protestants fighting a religious war with Catholics, believing that the Christian fights on his knees in prayer. Huldrych Zwingli disagreed and was killed outside Zurich as a chaplain for the Protestant army that fought against the Catholics. Church/state issues are complex, but history helps us define the issues.

By the end of our journey, we'll be encouraged to learn that God uses imperfect people in His work. We'll marvel at Luther's courage and be bewildered by his anger and personal vendettas. We'll be impressed with John Calvin's mind and yet question his wisdom in agreeing with the decision of the Geneva city council to have the heretic Michael Servetus burned at the stake. We'll be deeply disappointed in Zwingli for agreeing with the Zurich city council that those who rejected the doctrine of infant baptism (and therefore baptize one another as believers) should be put to death.

And yes, we'll learn that faith has a price tag. Whether it is John Hus burned for his beliefs at the Council of Constance or Felix Manz forcibly drowned in the Limmat river, we'll be surprised at the many thousands who were martyred for their faith. We'll be astonished at just how dark God allowed the world to become before the flickers were fanned into a flame in Germany that would eventually shine around the world.

On at least a half dozen occasions it's been my privilege to lead a tour to the sites of the Reformation in Germany and Switzerland. Each time the tours end, I leave more deeply committed to defend "the faith . . . once delivered unto the saints" (Jude 3 KJV). As you join me on this journey, I hope you'll be instructed, inspired, and determined to stand for the clarity of the gospel at any cost. Together we'll be intellectually stretched and spiritually enriched. We have to rescue the gospel from distortions, cheap substitutes, and neglect.

We will rediscover those truths that made the church great.

1

Power, Scandals, and Corruption

Christianity can survive without the gospel.

Let me clarify. There is a form of Christianity that developed in medieval times that has survived to this day without the gospel. It is, of course, a powerless Christianity that cannot give people the assurance of salvation, nor does it lead to lives of holiness—but it is still called *Christianity*. Yes, whether Catholic or Protestant, every generation, including ours, has to fight for the purity of the gospel. It's our nature to reject the gospel's verdict on us and resist the profound simplicity of its transforming message of grace. The gospel must always be defended, and sometimes it must be *rescued*.

By any estimation, at the close of the fifteenth century and the beginning of the sixteenth, the Catholic Church was in desperate need of reformation. Many of the church leaders were living in shameless decadence that bred cynicism among the common worshipers. Queen Isabella of Castile (1451–1504) wrote that the "majority of the clergy are living in open concubinage, and if our justice intervenes in order to punish them, they revolt and create a scandal, and that they despise our justice to the point that they arm themselves against it."[1]

Or consider this assessment of medieval Christianity by Andrea di Strumi. "At that time, however, the ecclesiastical order was corrupted by so many errors that hardly anyone could be found who was truly in his proper place. Some served the pleasures of the hunt, wandering about with hounds and hawks, others were tavern-keepers and wicked overseers . . . almost all led shameful lives either with wives who had been acknowledged publicly or with concubines."[2]

By this time, the gospel had been buried under centuries of traditions and superstitions. As one writer put it, "We had too many churches, too many relics (true and fake), too many untruthful miracles. Instead of worshiping the only living Lord, we worshiped dead bones; in the place of immortal Christ, we worshiped mortal bread [the consecrated bread of the mass]."[3]

As the power of the Catholic Church grew, so did the exaggerated claims of spiritual authority. Priests, who were taught that they had the power to turn ordinary bread and wine into the actual body and blood of Christ, believed that they could also withhold or grant salvation to whomever they wished. And certainly the pope could open heaven for his friends or send his enemies to hell. Clearly, the gospel needed to be rescued from the misleading traditions of medieval Christianity.

Even ardent Catholics will admit that the church needed reform—and needed it badly. They might wish that the reforms hadn't gone as far as they did under Luther, but they have to acknowledge that the church had been sliding into corruption for centuries and that the abuses needed to be halted.

The Babylonian Captivity of the Church

Let's review a bit of history. Consider this scandal. Beginning in 1305 and lasting until 1377 (a total of seventy-two years), there were six successive popes, all of French origin, ruling from Avignon in southern France. Can you imagine the reaction of the citizens of Rome to the humiliation that their city—believed for centuries to be the burial site of St. Peter's remains—no longer housed the papacy? This usurpation of authority was deeply resented not only in Italy but also in Germany. Since Rome refused to support the "rebel" papacy, the French popes raised money in any way they could, whether through taxes, wars, or bribery.

This period in church history is known as "The Babylonian Captivity of the Church" because the papacy was absent from Rome or held captive in France for seventy years (actually, seventy-two years), just as Israel was held captive in Babylon for seventy years.

The Italians were ecstatic when at last, in 1377, an Italian pope was elected and the papacy moved back to Rome. But now an even more embarrassing scandal erupted. The pope who had been ruling in Avignon refused to resign. Now there were *two* popes ruling simultaneously. And when both of them were deposed by the cardinals and a new pope elected, they both refused to accept the decision and step down. This resulted in *three* popes ruling at the same time. All three claimed to be the legitimate successor to Peter, calling the others "antichrist" and selling indulgences to make enough money to fight against the other two.

It wasn't until the Council of Constance in 1414 that all three popes stepped down and made room for one successor. The thirty-six-year period in which there were multiple rival popes (who weren't exactly role models of credibility and humility) is known as "The Papal Schism."

These scandals, of course, made the common people doubt that the papacy represented Christ, the head of the church. What's more, various countries in Europe sided with one pope or another, thus the confusion and corruption of the church was clear for all to see. Loyalty to the papacy was at the very least questioned if not altogether abandoned.

Yes, obviously, some people did understand and believe the gospel during these centuries of spiritual darkness and confusion. Monks who had access to the Scriptures often experienced personal devotion to Christ. The gospel, though buried under centuries of conflicting traditions, could be found by those who sought it out. God did not leave Himself without a witness.

Abuses Tolerated

Other abuses of power also haunted the church. Clergy who were brought to trial for one reason or another were tried by a tribunal of the church, not in civil courts. Today in the United States, priests are subject to our constitutional and civil laws, but in those days, they were tried by canon law as interpreted by their own peers. We can imagine the abuses that were tolerated by appointed churchmen who were more interested in protecting their colleagues and grasping for power than in acting for what was best for the people, or more important, what was honoring to God. The attempts by the church to cover its sins were obvious.

Simony (the selling of spiritual positions for money) was rampant. "Bishop bricks" were sold to the highest bidder. The legal recognition of Christianity under Constantine in the fourth century and the church's rise to wealth and power increased the temptation of church leaders to accept "gifts" in exchange for spiritual or sacred positions. Thus the church became wealthy

A twelfth-century painting showing an abbot selling a church position. The term "simony" derives from Simon Magus, who offered to buy the Holy Spirit from the apostles in Acts 8.

by acquiring lands and money, and as we might expect, the spiritual rulers who paid for their own promotions were often immoral and corrupt.

Parishioners were grateful that centuries earlier the church had decreed that the lifestyle of the priest did not affect the validity of the sacraments. Indeed, none other than the great theologian Augustine said that the sacraments had value *ex opere operato* ("out of the working of the works," or "in and of themselves"), even if the rituals were performed by "thieves and robbers." Therefore people need not fear that the sacraments they received were invalid. But for reasons that will be made clear later in this book, the common people were denied the privilege of hearing a gospel that would give them the assurance of eternal life. Doubt—often fearful doubt—about one's personal salvation was common and actually encouraged by the church. To be certain of one's personal salvation was considered to be the sin of presumption.

Long before Martin Luther arrived on the scene, ripples of reform weakened the monopoly the church had on people's souls. Thousands of people, both in England and continental Europe, knew that reform was long overdue and were ready to support it when it came. As we shall see, Luther stood on the shoulders of others who had affirmed the same doctrinal convictions that he would come to believe. Although the official church was able to squelch previous reform movements, it wasn't able to stem the

This illustration from a Czech manuscript depicts the devil selling indulgences nearly thirty years before Martin Luther published the *Ninety-Five Theses*.

tide started by Luther. The eventual break from Rome ignited under Luther was both final and irreversible.

In the next chapter, we'll look at two voices of reform that began a stream that eventually flowed into a larger river of reform under the leadership of Martin Luther. It's not too much to say that we cannot understand Luther unless we first grasp the impact of these two forerunners of the Reformation movement. Even Luther himself acknowledged that he stood on the shoulders of these giants of the faith.

2

A Morning Star
and a Goose and Swan

M any people think that the Reformation began when Martin Luther famously nailed his *Ninety-Five Theses* to the door of the Castle Church in Wittenberg. But his heroic efforts were preceded by a number of others who risked their lives to rescue the gospel from a church that was overrun by unscrupulous leaders, political intrigue, and doctrinal corruption.

These prereformers tried to reform the church before the period we commonly refer to as the Reformation, but their success was limited and generally confined to local areas or a few specific issues. And yet their attempts weakened the stranglehold that the church had on the masses and paved the way for Luther.

John Wycliffe: Morning Star of the Reformation (1330–84)

On one tour to the sites of the Reformation in England, we visited one of the most impressive churches in all of Europe: St. Paul's Cathedral in London. After attending a service, our group went to the northeast corner of the churchyard, where a statue of St. Paul of the Cross stands. It is, as you might guess, a monument in honor of St. Paul, after whom the cathedral is named. Centuries earlier at this very spot, copies of the English Bible were burned; in fact, the church awarded money to individuals who confiscated copies of the Scriptures so that they could be destroyed.

These Bibles were laboriously copied by followers of John Wycliffe, the man known as the "Morning Star of the Reformation" (a reference to Venus, the star that heralds the coming of dawn). Just so, Wycliffe led a revolt against the church that would be the first glimmer of light that would penetrate the spiritual darkness in England and the rest of Europe.

Who Was John Wycliffe?

Wycliffe was born in 1330 in the quaint little town of Ipreswell (modern Hipswell), England. He entered Oxford and was trained to preach. Since he was living during the days of "The Babylonian Captivity of the Church" and even during a few years of "The Papal Schism," he was well aware of the corruption of the church.

One of the great thinkers of his age, Wycliffe wrote important books on philosophy and theology. Quite simply, he was Oxford's leading theologian. Some of his ideas were radical and would have been impossible to implement. Aiming his ire at the corrupt clergy of England and the pope, he taught that those who rule unjustly are in breach of the terms under which God delegates authority. He espoused the radical belief that the government should have the right to seize land that belonged to corrupt clerics. Although such ideas were impractical, they had the effect of encouraging people to stand against the abuses perpetrated by the church.

The church in England was wealthy. It owned about a third of the land in England and yet paid no taxes. This upset Wycliffe. More to the point,

he argued that obedience to the
visible and often corrupt church
leaders was not necessary; what
mattered to God was the invisible
church of the elect. Rather than
looking to the pope or his emis-
saries, one just needed to study the
Bible to learn all that was necessary for the Christian life.

He also attacked the doctrine
of transubstantiation, the teaching that, at the command of the
priest, the substance of the bread

Statue of John Wycliffe in the Luther Memorial in Worms, Germany

and the wine are changed into the literal body and blood of Christ. He
believed that Christ was, in some sense, present in the bread and wine,
but he insisted that even after consecration, the bread remains bread,
and the wine remains wine. His view struck a blow to the power of the
clergy, who propagated the belief that they had the power to perform
this miracle of transformation.

The Primacy of the Bible

Wycliffe's greatest contribution to reform was to popularize the Bible.
In those days, for the most part only Latin translations were available,
which were inaccessible to most people; they were kept in churches and
read by the clergy, who were supposed to translate the text and teach
people its contents. Wycliffe believed that if the common people had a
Bible in their own language, the few who were able to read could then
read it to others, and the gospel could be rediscovered.

His was not the best English translation because it was translated
from the Latin Vulgate. But despite its imperfections, it gave the

people a more accurate reading of the contents of the New Testament than what they'd been hearing from the clergy. Most interesting for our study, Wycliffe believed that the Scripture was complete—it contained the whole of God's revelation. Thus canon law, church tradition, and even the papacy had to be judged by Scripture. There was no need for unscriptural traditions, nor did the church need a pope to rule over it. Christ was the only head that the church needed.

Wycliffe believed that the papacy was of human origin, so when he was condemned by Pope Gregory XI with eighteen bulls (papal

Wycliffe inspired and oversaw the translation of the Bible from the Latin Vulgate into English. He likely translated the New Testament himself, and his associates translated the Old Testament.

decrees), he disregarded the threats and charges of heresy. In fact, as far as Wycliffe was concerned, the pope was antichrist.

The church, in turn, argued that if the common people read the Bible, they would conjure up all kinds of strange interpretations. But Wycliffe was willing to take the risk, believing that they might also come to understand the gospel and thus be saved. So he wanted the Bible to be read by as many people as possible—clergy and the common people alike.

Keep in mind that this was before Gutenberg's printing press, so all the Bibles were hand copied. It took one scribe ten months to copy a Bible, so we can imagine that making hundreds of them needed the work of hundreds of people. The fact that there are still 170 of Wycliffe's

Bibles in existence today proves that many were copied, and thankfully, the ecclesiastical powers did not find all of them.

Wycliffe's Followers

Wycliffe's disciples were called Lollards, and although the meaning of the term has been lost, the best guess is that it meant "mumblers"; that is, it was a term of derision given to Wycliffe's disciples by those who hated them. It's also been suggested that it meant "vagabonds" or that it was taken from the Latin word for "tares in the wheat." In any case, it was a term of scorn and contempt for those who followed Wycliffe.

The Lollards suffered greatly for their faith. Near Lambeth Palace in London (the London residence of the archbishop of Canterbury) is the Lollard Tower. It was so named because it was there that so many of the Lollard martyrs were imprisoned. And nearby, in the Lambeth fields, Christians were slaughtered for their faith.

But John Wycliffe prepared his pupils for persecution and even martyrdom. His curriculum included such topics as how to live a life of sparse existence, how to refute a priest's arguments, and how to be willing to die for the faith. His followers were so faithful that 145 years after his own death, Lollards were still in existence.

Though Wycliffe was slated to be killed, he collapsed while speaking and died a few days later on December 28, 1384. Hence, he cheated the ecclesiastical powers by denying them the privilege of killing him. However, over thirty years after his death, at the Council of Constance (see discussion below), the decision was made to dig up his bones, burn them, and throw the ashes into the Swift River. The superstitious belief was that if his bones were destroyed, it would spoil his chances at a resurrection.

History has shown that there is real continuity between the Lollards and the later Protestant Reformation. In giving people the Bible and

Wycliffe Giving "The Poor Priests" His Translation of the Bible by William Frederick Yeames

stirring discontent with the papacy, the seeds were sown for much wider and more drastic reforms. And as we shall see, Wycliffe's impact was felt all the way to Prague, where another courageous reformer took what he learned and began the process of transforming a city.

Unlike Wycliffe, this man was burned at the stake.

John Hus: The Goose That Became a Swan (1369–1415)

Reform movements spawn other reform movements, and soon the ideas of John Wycliffe spread beyond England to continental Europe. The Holy Roman emperor Charles IV established a university in Prague in 1348. And in a gesture of goodwill, his daughter Anne married King Richard II of England, bringing the two countries into an alliance of friendship. As a result, Czech students were invited to study at Oxford, where they encountered the teachings of Wycliffe. They took his ideas back to Prague along with some of his writings. Some people condemned Wycliffe while others defended him, but it wasn't long before a growing desire to reform the church was fueled by his writings. One of the men who was greatly influenced by Wycliffe's teachings was John Hus, who would later become a famous reformer in Prague.

Who Was John Hus?

Hus was born to poor parents (c. 1369), but despite their poverty, he was able to graduate from the University of Prague and eventually taught there. He had read John Wycliffe's writings, and though he rejected the more radical ideas, he agreed that the clergy were corrupt and needed reform. So he began to preach Reformation ideas in Prague's Bethlehem Chapel.

He decried the doctrine of relics, the idea that there are certain benefits given to those who pay a gift to view them. In other words, he rejected the notion that if someone touched something that was in the possession of a martyr—a wisp of hair, a piece of clothing—special grace was imparted from the martyr in heaven to the worshiper on earth. Hus taught that giving a "gift" for such a privilege denied the doctrine of grace.

Then there was the matter of indulgences. If you paid a certain amount of money, you could purchase a document that guaranteed that you would be free from the temporal consequences of sin. This doctrine, taught for centuries, was becoming increasingly corrupt in its solicitation of funds for the clergy.

Like Wycliffe, Hus argued that the Bible alone was the basis for spiritual authority—not the church, not councils, not traditions—and if the Bible is sufficient for spiritual guidance, it should be available to everyone.

Although the writings of Wycliffe were officially condemned in Prague, Hus, who shared the core of Wycliffe's beliefs, was appointed as the rector of the university. When the pope heard of this, Hus was banned from preaching in Bethlehem Chapel, where he often preached twice a day to an ever-widening circle of listeners. Hus refused to obey the pope and was therefore excommunicated by his archbishop. In the same year that two hundred of Wycliffe's books were publicly burned in England, Hus was summoned to Rome. He wisely refused to go and sent representatives in his stead.

More Indulgences

Hus's anger was stirred when Pope John XXIII launched a crusade against the king of Naples. In order to recruit soldiers, the pope offered them full remission of sins if they joined his effort; in other words, their sacrifice was their payment for indulgences. Hus was outraged at the thought of using spiritual blessings in exchange for political gain and

A seventeenth-century papal bull. The document is called a "bull" because of the lead *bulla* (Latin for "seal") that authenticates the document.

attacked this form of simony. The population of Prague agreed and rose in rebellion by ceremonially burning a papal bull (official papal document) that granted indulgences.

As a result of this reform activity, the pope put the city of Prague under an interdict, which meant that sacraments could not be performed in the city—no baptisms, masses, last rites, marriages, or the like. And since most of the people believed that without the sacraments hell awaited them, they rose up against Hus so that the pope would restore the sacraments.

Keep in mind that the church taught that only the priests could administer the sacraments, which were necessary for heaven; thus, the priests held the salvation of their parishioners in their own hands. To be cut off from the church was equivalent to being cut off from God.

There were some people who supported Hus, but only for political reasons. The Bohemians wanted to be free from German influence, so they viewed Hus as a representative of Czech nationalism. They thought his reforms would lead to national independence from the church and its political powers, and years later, many people followed Martin Luther for the same reason.

Given the uproar over the interdict, Hus chose to leave the city and went to south Bohemia where he wrote two of his most important books: *The Church* and *Simony*. He also preached far and wide, extending his circle of influence.

In his book *The Church*, he defined the church as the body of Christ, with Christ alone its head. Although he defended the authority of the clergy, he taught that God could forgive sin without the necessity of a priest. He believed that the true church coexisted with the false church in this life (the wheat and the tares grow together). He said that Christians need not obey an order unless it was found in Scripture. He criticized the people for worshiping images, believing in false miracles, and taking spiritual pilgrimages. He disagreed with the teaching that the wine at communion should be withheld from the laity, and as already mentioned, he attacked the sale of indulgences. Simply put, he believed that there was a difference between obeying God and obeying a heretical church.

Having found refuge from the turmoil in Prague by being invited to stay in the castle of King Wenceslas in Krakovec, Hus continued to expand his influence through his writings. But soon his life would take a critical turn.

Trouble at the Council

The Council of Pisa met in 1409 to resolve the embarrassment of "The Papal Schism" when two popes were ruling simultaneously. As already mentioned, when they deposed both of the ruling popes and elected Alexander V, the deposed popes refused to resign, resulting in three popes ruling simultaneously. All three were fighting each other, all claiming to be the rightful heir of Peter's chair. This council was widely condemned because it was unable to put an end to the scandal.

Obviously, something had to be done. Meanwhile, a new emperor was ruling in Europe. Emperor Sigismund, younger brother of Prague's King Wenceslas, wanted to enhance his prestige, so he called a special council that met at Constance, Germany (1414–18). On the agenda, of course, was the immediate issue of bringing an end to the "The Papal Schism," and then there was the matter of dealing with heresy.

For openers, the council at Constance had to declare that it had more authority than the papacy so that their decision about the disarray of the papacy would be binding. They deposed all three popes and elected Martin V as the new pope. Thankfully, two of the other three popes eventually resigned, but the third, Pope John XXIII, was at the council still hoping that he could muster support for his papal authority. When he saw that his bid to be the sole pope was rejected, he fled the council but was arrested. At any rate, the church now had only one pope, and the embarrassment of "The Papal Schism" was over.

Interestingly, the newly elected pope, Martin V, later repudiated the notion that the council had authority over the papacy, thus gaining total independence and supremacy. I'm sure he appreciated the authority of the council when it elected him as pope, but that's where their authority ended and his began!

But the work of the council was not yet finished; there was the matter of heresy that still had to be dealt with. The emperor was determined that the heretical teachings of Hus had to be suppressed.

The Burning of Hus

John Hus was invited to attend the Council of Constance to face charges of heresy. The emperor promised him safe-conduct to and from the council, and he was to be protected even if his condemnation by the church was not reversed. With great hesitation and with the urging of King Wenceslas, Hus reluctantly agreed to go. As word got out that he was en route to Constance, his trip through Germany turned into a triumphal procession. It was apparent that the German people were also ripe for reform.

Weeks after his arrival, Hus was put on trial and found guilty of heresy. Although he had successfully repudiated the charge that he agreed with all of Wycliffe's writings, the judges nevertheless extracted forty-two articles from his book on the church that were in conflict with official ecclesiastical teaching. Thus he was condemned as a heretic.

By now, Hus had been transferred to the castle in Gottlieben, across the border in eastern Switzerland. He was given very little food and water in an attempt to break his spirit. He also spent time in a horrible hole of a cell in a monastery on an island just offshore. When he was brought to trial, he said he would be glad to recant if it could be shown that his views were contrary to Scripture. Three years before his death, he said, "I have said that I would not, for a chapel full of gold, recede from the truth. . . . I know that the truth stands and is mighty for ever, and abides eternally, with whom there is no respect of persons."[1]

His letters, written to friends back in Prague, are very touching. "O most holy Christ," he prayed, "draw me, weak as I am, after Thyself, for if Thou dost not draw us we cannot follow Thee. Strengthen my spirit, that it may be willing. If the flesh is weak, let Thy grace precede us; come between and follow, for without Thee we cannot go for Thy sake to a cruel death. Give me a fearless heart, a right faith, a firm hope, a perfect love, that for Thy sake I may lay down my life with patience and joy, Amen."[2]

The emperor agreed with the council that it was not necessary to keep his promise to a heretic. Hus received no apology for a broken promise of safe passage, nor was he given another opportunity to defend himself.

Hus made his final declaration to the council on July 1, 1415, five days before his death. He said that he was not willing to recant, then added, "And if it were possible that my voice could now reach the whole

John Hus is burned at the stake.

world, as at the Day of Judgment every lie and every sin that I have committed will be made manifest, then would I gladly abjure [recant] before all the world every falsehood and error which I either had thought of saying or actually said!"[3]

Finally, on July 6, 1415, the day of his burning came. He was brought into the cathedral where Emperor Sigismund, dressed in full regalia, was sitting on the throne. The charges against Hus were summarized, and when he protested the facts, he was told to keep quiet. After being instructed to stand on a table, he was mocked and cursed. A tall paper crown was placed on his head. The crown was painted with three devils fighting for the possession of a soul and the words "The Chief of Heretics."

The bishops committed his soul to the devil, but Hus replied, "And I commit it to the most merciful Lord Jesus Christ."[4] Sigismund then turned him over to the executioners. King Wenceslas, who had been a friend of Hus but was also the brother of the emperor, did nothing to prevent the execution.

On the way to the execution, Hus saw a bonfire of his books. He laughed and told the bystanders not to believe the lies that were told about him. When he arrived at the place where he would be put to death, he knelt and prayed. For the last time, he was asked if he would recant. He replied, "God is my witness that the evidence against me is false. I have never thought nor preached except with the one intention of winning men, if possible, from their sins. In the truth of the gospel I have written, taught, and preached; today I will gladly die."[5]

They disrobed him, tied his hands behind his back, then bound his neck to the stake with a rusty chain. He commented with a smile that his Savior had been bound by a heavier chain. When the fire was lit, Hus began to sing, "Christ, Thou Son of the living God, have mercy on us," then, "Christ, Thou Son of the living God have mercy on me."[6] He began a prayer he did not finish, for the wind blew the flame into his face.

The Goose Was Cooked

The word *hus* in Czech is the word for *goose*. A priest who watched the execution reported that before Hus died, he said, "You can cook this goose [Hus] but within a century a swan shall arise who will prevail."

Evidently the swan was thought of as a special bird; in fact it later became a symbol of the Christian faith in the Netherlands.

A century later, Martin Luther saw himself as the fulfillment of Hus's prophecy. He said, "Holy Johannes Hus prophesied about me when he wrote from his Bohemian prison that they might now be roasting a goose [Hus], but in a hundred years they will hear a swan sing, which they will not be able to silence. And that is the way it will be, if God wills."[7] And 102 years after Hus was martyred, Luther nailed his *Ninety-Five Theses* to the door of the Castle Church in Wittenberg.

But let's return to the Council of Constance. It was not enough to kill a living man; it was also apparently necessary to exhume a dead one. They not only condemned the writings of John Wycliffe in England; they also demanded that his body be exhumed and his ashes thrown into the Swift River. But, as has often been pointed out, the Swift River flows into the Avon, and the Avon eventually flows into the Severn, which flows to the Bristol Channels and then into the oceans of the world. Thus, the teaching of Wycliffe and the Bible he popularized flowed from one river to the next and eventually into the entire world. Hus and his followers are the most obvious example of the fact that persecution cannot stamp out the influence of the gospel.

The Impact of Hus

The church had offered the people of Bohemia a martyr. The reform movement survived, but it divided into two groups. Some members of the majority wanted only minor reforms of the Roman Catholic system. Their chief demand was that the laity also receive the cup and not just the bread when the mass was conducted.

Others would be content only with a more thorough reform. When they were persecuted, some joined with other reform groups such as the Waldensians (the followers of Peter Waldo). A century later, when

Luther began his reform in Germany, many who remained loyal to Hus's reforms (the church of the Brethren, for example) joined his movement.

John Hus also planted the seeds for the Moravian church that was later led by a man named Ludwig Zinzendorf. It was under his leadership that the Moravians sent 265 missionaries around the world in the eighteenth century. The great English evangelist John Wesley was converted largely because of Moravian influence. And so the impact of Wycliffe, Hus, and those who followed them continued in diverse but memorable ways.

As for Martin Luther, he initially denied he was a follower of Hus, but after studying Hus's writings more carefully, he admitted with gratitude, "I am a Hussite." Luther affirmed this knowing full well that Hus was burned at the stake and that he (Luther) could expect a similar fate—but he ended up being the swan they couldn't silence.

His story is captivating, instructive, and relevant for today.

3

The Wittenberg Door

When Martin Luther walked the half mile from his home in Wittenberg to the Castle Church, he was angry. He was about to nail a list of challenges against certain Catholic teachings to the church door, which also served as a bulletin board in the small town. He intended to spark a debate over the abuses that he believed existed in the church of his day.

He was angry, and with good reason.

In Rome, Pope Leo X was squandering the resources of the church on carnivals, war, gambling, and hunting. Even the pope's friends and advisers were uncomfortable with the excesses of the pontiff, who is reported to have jovially remarked, "The Lord has given [the papacy] to us—let us enjoy it!"[1] Catholic historian Ludwig von Pastor declared that "the ascent of this man in an hour of crisis to the chair of St. Peter . . . was one of the most severe trials to which God ever subjected his Church."[2] Eventually, this pope would preside over a church that would be so ripe for reform that when Luther summoned others to join him in condemning the abuses, tens of thousands would readily agree, and the church would be torn apart.

Pope Leo's problem can be simply stated: he needed money to complete the new St. Peter's Basilica in Rome. The old one, dating back to the time of Constantine in about AD 319, had been condemned. Under the leadership of Pope Julius II, a new basilica was

Pope Leo X was born Giovanni de Medici and was an extravagant patron of the arts.

begun. The piers of the new basilica were laid, but when Julius died, the project was left unfinished. Pope Leo wanted to finish it, so a deal was reached by which the empty coffers of the papacy could be filled and the basilica completed.

A man named Albert of Brandenburg aspired to become the archbishop of Mainz. Even before he was old enough to be an archbishop, he already held two bishoprics, but to hold a third was illegal. He knew that the cost to buy this third honor would be high.

Albert and the pope haggled about the price. As historian Roland Bainton put it, "The pope demanded twelve thousand ducats [gold coins] for the twelve apostles. Albert offered seven thousand for the seven deadly sins. They compromised on ten thousand, presumably not for the Ten Commandments."[3]

Now that the price was agreed to, the next step was for Albert to come up with the money. Since he had to pay the entire amount up front before he could assume office, he turned to the German bank for a loan with the understanding, of course, that the funds would be repaid. For Albert to repay the loan to the bank and for the pope to get funds, they struck a deal. The bank would advance money to pay what Albert owed the pope, giving the papacy some much-needed cash. In return, the pope would authorize the sale of indulgences in Albert's territories, the proceeds of which would be split between what Albert owed the bank and the papacy. So the pope would have his initial ten thousand ducats and continuous income to move the project forward.

Indulgences were therefore sold throughout Albert's territories with the promise that enough money would be raised to repay his debt, and the construction on St. Peter's Basilica could continue. Even today we marvel at St. Peter's Basilica's size and opulence. Although updates and additions have been made since the 1500s, the tall central building owes its existence in large part to the day when indulgences were sold to pay for its construction.

Indulgences: Then and Now

Indulgences have a long history in the development of Christianity. Among some pagan practices, a gift was sometimes received as a substitute for punishment for an offense. The church borrowed this idea and often received money in place of the punishment one should have received as a consequence for sins.

Even in the early centuries when persecution came to the church and some Christians denied the faith under pressure, most church leaders insisted that those who wished to return to the church had to prove their sincere repentance by doing prescribed good deeds. To readmit them back into the church without a penalty seemed to smack of what we would call "easy believism."

This idea that sinners should give evidence of their remorse was treated in various ways throughout the early centuries of Christianity, but eventually the church solidified its views. Yes, good deeds should be done as a due penalty for sin, but if a person could not perform good deeds or if they wished to give a "gift" instead, this contribution was gladly received. Eventually, any contribution prescribed by the church was deemed valid. Your "gift" was seen as a payment or penalty for committing a particular sin.

Indulgences were (and still are) a part of the sacrament of penance. After contrition, satisfaction, and prayers for forgiveness, there was still the matter of the temporal consequences of sin that needed to be addressed, and this was done by the payment of a gift. An indulgence, therefore, became known as an action by a church leader(s) that removed the temporal penalty for an individual's sin.

The updated *Catechism of the Catholic Church* (1995 edition) defines an indulgence as "a remission before God of the temporal punishment due to sins whose guilt has already been forgiven. . . . An indulgence is partial or plenary according as it removes either part or all of the temporal punishment due to sin. Indulgences may be applied to the living or the dead."[4] Then what follows is a discussion of the distinction between mortal sin—which, if not addressed, leads to eternal punishment—and venial sin—which, if not purified here on earth, leads to purgatory.

Portrait of Martin Luther by Lucas Cranach the Elder, 1529

Strictly speaking, an indulgence cannot forgive sin; only God can do that. An indulgence can only cancel the temporal consequences of sin; it was a penalty for having committed a sin and a warning that all sin is costly and should not be repeated. Unfortunately, some parishioners began to calculate how much a particular sin might cost them and often concluded that committing it might be worth the penalty.

Notice that the definition above says that it can also be applied to the dead because, after all, purgatory itself is seen as a temporal penalty for sin. The reasoning goes like this: Although most people at death are too good to go to hell (most don't die with mortal sin), they are nonetheless not good enough to go to heaven. Therefore, in the fires of purgatory, their sins are purged, and they are made ready for heaven. Although theologians distinguished between the penalty due to sin (which required an indulgence) and the guilt of sin (which only God could forgive), the common person saw no distinction, so they viewed an indulgence as a ticket to heaven.

Indulgences continue to be a part of Catholic theology. When Pope Francis visited Brazil for World Youth Day in 2013, the Vatican offered a plenary (complete) indulgence to those who could not attend the event but followed it on social media. The official pronouncement read:

> The faithful who on account of a legitimate impediment cannot attend the aforementioned celebrations may obtain Plenary Indulgence [full indulgence] under the usual spiritual, sacramental, and prayer conditions, in a spirit of filial submission to the Roman Pontiff, by participation in the sacred functions on the days indicated, following the same rites and spiritual exercises as they occur via television or radio or, with due devotion, via the new means of social communication.[5]

The Vatican confirmed that the faithful could follow the events on Twitter, the internet, or other means. The difference between today and days gone by is that no "gift" is stipulated. Simply following the rituals and showing proper devotion to God is enough to receive this benefit. On a visit to Rome, I saw that indulgences could also be obtained by performing various spiritual rituals, such as praying a prayer on each step of the Scala Sancta (Holy Stairs), burning incense in certain churches, and so forth. Indulgences weren't just rampant during Luther's time; they are still an important doctrine in Catholic theology today.

All Saints' Day

Frederick the Wise, a prince who ruled in a territory of Saxony that included Wittenberg where Luther was a professor, did not allow the pope's indulgences to be sold in his territory. He had his own indulgences sold in the town every November 1—All Saints' Day. Although the pope's vendors were not welcome in Saxony, the people of Wittenberg simply crossed the Elbe River to buy their indulgences.

Albert had briefed the pope's vendors on how to sell the approved indulgences in order to get the most money from the peasants. Those who paid the prescribed amount were promised that they would enjoy a plenary (full) and perfect remission of all sins. They could be restored to a state of innocence, which they enjoyed in baptism, and would be relieved of the pains of purgatory. In fact, the living could buy indulgences for the dead to exempt them from the fires of purgatory; for the right price, the souls of relatives or friends could enter heaven.

The most dedicated vendor was the Dominican friar Johann Tetzel. When he approached a town, he was met by dignitaries who attended him in a solemn procession. A cross bearing the papal arms preceded him, and the pope's bull (the official declaration) was borne aloft on a gold-embroidered cushion. The cross was planted in the town square, and then the sermon began.

> Consider the salvation of your souls and those of your departed loved ones. . . . Visit the holy cross erected before you. . . . Listen to the voices of your dear dead relatives and friends beseeching you and saying, "Pity us, pity us. We are in dire torment from which you can redeem us for a

pittance." Do you not wish to? Open your ears. Hear the father saying to his son, the mother to her daughter, "We bore you, nourished you, brought you up, left you our fortunes, and you are so cruel and hard that now you are not willing for so little to set us free. Will you let us lie here in flames? Will you delay our promised glory?"[6]

Then followed a jingle, which can be translated from the German:

> As soon as the coin in the coffer rings,
> Another soul from purgatory springs.

The people of Wittenberg who bought these indulgences returned with pardons in their hand. They reported that the cross Tetzel brought to the town's square was of equal value to the cross of Christ. In fact, some people bought indulgences for sins that they had not yet committed but intended to commit![7]

The *Ninety-Five Theses*

For Martin Luther, this was the last straw. And so it was that on October 31, 1517, he posted his *Ninety-Five Theses* to the door of the Castle Church in Wittenberg. He had no intention of breaking from the church; the idea that his actions would eventually change the map of Europe didn't even enter his mind. In fact, he wasn't even opposed to indulgences but only wished to correct their abuses. "This act,

The church door at Wittenberg was used as a bulletin board for theological discussion.

far from being an act of rebellion was actually the act of a dutiful son of mother church."[8]

Luther intended to debate the issue locally, not realizing that he would eventually tap into the growing sentiment that the church cared more about money than it did souls. He attacked the practice of indulgences, saying that it would be better to build "living temples" than for the Germans to invest their money in a new basilica that meant nothing for them. But money aside, Luther's greatest anger was directed

The present Castle Church door has the *Ninety-Five Theses* engraved in Latin. Above the door is a relief of Luther (with an open Bible) and Melanchthon (with a copy of the Augsburg Confession) bowing before the crucified Christ.

toward the misleading notion that sins could be forgiven through the purchase of indulgences.

The preamble to the *Ninety-Five Theses* reads, "Out of love and zeal for truth and the desire to bring it to light, the following theses will be publicly discussed at Wittenberg under the chairmanship of the reverend father Martin Luther." The following is a sample of what the theses said.

> *Thesis 1.* When our Lord and Master Jesus Christ said, "Repent," He willed the entire life of believers to be one of repentance.
>
> *Thesis 32.* Those who believe that they can be certain of their salvation because they have indulgence letters will be eternally damned, together with their teachers.
>
> *Thesis 52.* It is vain to trust in salvation by indulgence letters, even though the indulgence commissary, or even the pope, were to offer his soul as security.

Thesis 79. To say that the cross emblazoned with the papal coat of arms, and set up by the indulgence preachers, is equal in worth to the cross of Christ is blasphemy.

Thesis 82. Why does not the pope empty purgatory for the sake of holy love and the dire need of the souls that are there if he redeems an infinite number of souls for the sake of miserable money with which to build a church?[9]

Let me again emphasize that Luther himself did not condemn indulgences as such. He felt, however, that they had been abused. He was insistent that forgiveness could not be achieved by paying a gift, saying prayers, or being given a letter of indulgence.

Luther wrote his *Ninety-Five Theses* in Latin, intending that it be read only by the scholars with whom he hoped to debate the issues. But soon they were translated from Latin into German, and thanks to Gutenberg, printing presses were available in most of the cities of Germany. Copies were printed quickly and secretly. Within months they became the talk of Germany, and soon, much of Europe had read them. A copy was even given to Albert of Mainz, who was understandably very displeased with the contents.

Albert, in turn, forwarded a copy to Rome. Pope Leo, it is said, responded, "Luther is a drunken German. He will feel different when he is sober."[10] If the pope had corrected most of the most obvious abuses, Luther might have been satisfied. He was a busy professor and parish priest and had little desire for controversy. But the pope's response was to appoint a new general of the Augustinians so that he might "quench a monk of his order, Martin Luther by name, and thus smother the fire before it should become a conflagration."[11]

But the fire could not be smothered. In less than a year, Luther would be involved in two disputations (debates) that would further solidify his opposition to the system of salvation by works. Meanwhile, he gave himself to further study and writing, clarifying his views and spreading them with the help of the printing press.

Luther found himself in the middle of an ecclesiastical storm, a tempest whose speed and size increased week by week. He was caught up in a controversy far beyond what he had envisioned. Friends encouraged him; enemies rose up against him.

But why did he come to the growing realization that the church and popes could err? And how did he find the salvation that finally brought peace to his troubled soul? It is to these questions we now turn.

4

Who Was Martin Luther?

Pope Leo X called Luther "a wild boar in the vineyard of the Lord." Some devout Catholics believed he was possessed, and after he died, rumors circulated in Rome that demons left his body. His friends described him as a prophet who, like Elijah, went to heaven in a chariot. A more modest evaluation is that he was a reformer who rescued the gospel, which had been buried under centuries of tradition.

But regardless of the welter of opinions that surrounded Martin Luther, all agree that he left behind a Europe that was permanently changed. Countless books have been written about him. Some popes and emperors are remembered in history primarily because of their relationship with him. Whether they have loved or hated him, both Catholics and Protestants have been influenced by this remarkable man.

Luther's Background

There was nothing in Luther's background to suggest greatness. He was born into the humble home of Hans and Margarette Luther in Eisleben, Germany, on November 10, 1483, and named Martin because he was born on St. Martin's Day. His parents were pious and strict, so his home life was filled with a mixture of love and harsh discipline. His mother beat his hands until they bled for taking a nut from the kitchen table. His father spent his days working in a copper mine, and although he earned more money than most, Luther recalled that his mother still had to go into the forest to fetch wood. Prayer, strict morality, and loyalty to the traditions of the church were fervently expected.

Luther's early education was by rote, and although he respected his teachers, discipline was exceedingly strict by our standards. Instruction was given in Latin, and those who lapsed into German were given the rod. Religion was a part of everyday life, whether at home or at school. The presence of churches was everywhere with the ringing of bells, the adoration of relics, and the recitation of prayers.

In those early years, Luther experienced periods of depression, already well aware that he was a sinner who needed relief from the demons that seemed to plague him. Even when he enrolled in the University of Erfurt to study law, he was not free from his sensitive conscience, which reminded him that he was a sinner who needed to find a way to become right with God.

In July of 1505, he was caught in the middle of a thunderstorm, and when a lightning bolt struck the ground near him, he cried out, "St. Anne, help me! I will become a monk!" And so it was—partly to fulfill this vow and, most assuredly, because of his own inner turmoil—that Luther went against his father's wishes, left the university in Erfurt, and entered the Augustinian monastery in the same city. Now his course of study would switch from philosophy and law to a religious regimen that would, he hoped, satisfy the longings of his soul. Within the cloister, he thought, he'd find the answer to his depression and melancholic temperament.

Life as an Augustinian

In the monastery, the path to salvation was difficult but not impossible. The monks were reminded that purgatory existed for those who were not bad enough for hell or good enough for heaven. God was portrayed as angry and merciful, vengeful and forgiving. But if one followed the teachings of the church and took advantage of its many means of grace, one could reasonably hope that a merciful God would receive the penitent. All that anyone could do as they approached death was to appeal to Mary, asking that God would show some leniency and saving grace.

Luther was terror stricken at the thought of Christ as judge. He sought to lay hold of every means of grace that was available to him. He knew that he could never get to heaven without the merit of Christ, but he also believed that he had to earn such merit. Therefore, the only wise course of action was to pursue religion with all of his strength so that he might be worthy of God's grace. As a monk, he thought he had a better chance of saving his soul—especially if he died in the cowl, because then he might be given preferential treatment. Thus Luther committed himself to the most rigorous discipline in order that he might die with saving grace.

Meanwhile, he knew that his father was enraged by his decision to become a monk. Though Hans was later reconciled to his son, he was deeply disappointed that his brilliant boy did not study law and enjoy a salary that might help the family. But for Martin, the call of God on his life was more critical than pleasing his father. Making money was not nearly as important as the salvation of his tortured soul.

Luther and the other would-be monks would prostrate themselves on the steps of the altar at the grave of a man named Johannes Zachariae. And when the monks were asked, "What seekest thou?" they answered,

"God's grace and mercy." The rigors of monastic life were explained, which included "the renunciation of self-will, the scant diet, rough clothing, vigils by night and labors by day, mortification of the flesh, the reproach of poverty, the shame of begging, and the distastefulness of cloistered existence."[1]

With God's help, Luther promised to take these burdens upon himself. The choir sang, and civilian clothes were exchanged for the monk's habit. "Hear, O Lord, our heartfelt pleas and deign to confer thy blessing on this thy servant," intoned the prior, "that he may continue with thy help faithful in thy Church and merit eternal life through Jesus Christ our Lord. Amen."[2] Luther was then shown his cell, and he set out on a journey to make his peace with God.

Interestingly, Johannes Zachariae, who is buried at the altar where Luther and the other monks took their vows, played a significant part in the burning of Hus at the Council of Constance. Let's not skip over the irony: at the very altar that honors the memory of one who advocated the burning of Hus, there arose a second Hus who would shake the church to its foundations. As we learned in chapter 2, when Hus was about to be burned, he said, "You can cook this goose [Hus] but within a century a swan shall arise who will prevail." Now this "swan" (Luther) would eventually break the vows he was making and end up calling himself a "Hussite." He would be condemned as a heretic just as Hus had been.

Luther joined the Augustinian order in 1505, twelve years before he wrote the *Ninety-Five Theses*.

After the first probationary year ended, Luther was formally accepted into the monastic order. Prayers came seven times daily; after seven or eight hours of sleep, the monks were awakened between 1:00 and 2:00 in the morning by the ringing of the cloister bell. They jumped up, made the sign of the cross, donned their robes, and went into the church, where they sprinkled holy water on their heads. After appropriate prayers and chanting, the devotional time always ended with "Save, O Queen, Thou Mother of mercy, our life, our delight, and our hope. To Thee we exiled sons of Eve lift up our cry. To Thee we sigh as we languish in this vale of tears. Be Thou our advocate. Sweet Virgin Mary, pray for us. Thou holy Mother of God."[3]

In the monastery, at least for a time, Luther was confident that he was walking the path of the saints. And yet the more he fulfilled his duties, the more troubled his mind and heart became. He suffered from a depression born of guilt and despair—the humble realization that he was not yet meeting the demands of a righteous God. He suffered from *Anfechtungen*, an existential despair of the soul. (The German word may be interpreted as "guilt, fear, and isolation from God.")

His First Mass

Though prepared for his first mass as a priest, he hardly anticipated the terror that struck him as he said the words that transformed the wine into blood and the bread into the very flesh of Christ. He knew that performing this miracle was the high point of priestly worship. Only priests had such power; this teaching lay at the heart of the distinction between the laity and the clergy. Only a priest ordained of God could take these ordinary elements and make them *extra*ordinary—only they could transform them into the literal flesh and blood of Christ. After the transformation, the church taught that these elements were "God of very God," and hence worthy of worship.

Luther postponed the date of his first mass because he wanted his father to be present. They hadn't seen each other since his days at the university. And though Hans had overcome his resentment triggered by his son's entrance into the monastery, he grudgingly sought reconciliation. When the day of his son's first mass came, Hans arrived at the monastery with an entourage of twenty horsemen.

Before approaching the altar, the younger Luther received absolution for all of his sins. His vestments were carefully arranged. No mistake, however, was to be regarded as fatal, since the church taught that the efficacy of the sacrament depended only on the right intention to perform it. Luther took his place before the altar and began to recite the introductory portion until he came to the words, "We offer unto thee, the living, the true, the eternal God." Afterward, he related,

> At these words I was utterly stupefied and terror-stricken. I thought to myself, "With what tongue shall I address such Majesty, seeing that all men ought to tremble in the presence of even an earthly prince? Who am I, that I should lift up mine eyes or raise my hands to the divine Majesty? The angels surround him. At his nod the earth trembles. And shall I, a miserable little pygmy, say, 'I want this, I ask for that?' For I am dust and ashes and full of sin and I am speaking to the living, eternal and the true God."[4]

Only by fearful restraint could he complete the mass. His was the fear of ancient Israel before the ark of the Lord; his was the fear of Sinai, the fear of the holy God whose vengeance is merciless and, for those who die with mortal sin, eternal. Luther felt the full weight of his sin, the painful reality that he, a sinful "pygmy," was standing in the presence of a holy God.

Later, over a meal, Luther turned to his father in hopes of making reconciliation. "Dear father, why were you so contrary to my becoming a monk? And perhaps you are not quite satisfied even now. The life is so quiet and godly." With this, Hans flared up before all the doctors and masters, "You learned scholar, have you never read in the Bible that you should honor your father and your mother? And here you have left me and your dear mother to look after ourselves in our old age."[5] He assured his father that he could do him more good by prayers than if he had earned money as a lawyer.

When Luther told his father that he had been called by the voice of God in the form of a thunderbolt, Hans replied, "God grant it was not an apparition of the devil." The day would come when Luther would indeed wonder whether he had heard God or the devil. But we're ahead of the story.

In Pursuit of Salvation

Luther gave himself without reservation to pursing the counsels of perfection. He fasted so often that his friends feared for his life; he practiced vigils and prayers in excess of those stipulated by the monastery. He often slept without blankets to mortify the flesh. He went begging to experience humiliation. Later he would write, "If I had kept on any longer, I should have killed myself with vigils, prayers, reading, and other work."[6] His problem was that he could not satisfy God at any point.

He hoped that he could find peace by adding the merit of the saints to his own disciplines. Goodness, the church taught, can be pooled. Some of the saints were better than they had to be to achieve their own salvation. As a result, a treasury of merit had accumulated, and these benefits were transferable to those who found themselves indebted to God. These benefits, the church said, extend even to the dead.

The church dispensed these merits to those who visited the relics of the saints. In fact, popes sometimes specified exactly how many years could be subtracted from the fires of purgatory by knowing which relics were viewed. And if this act was accompanied by a gift to the church, the merit to the worshiper would be increased.

The Journey to Rome

In 1510, Luther made a trip to Rome to settle a dispute in the Augustinian order. Imagine the distance he and his companion walked, staying in monasteries along the way. We who travel by cars, buses, and airplanes would do well to look at a map to see the route they had to take as they trekked through about 1,300 kilometers (800 miles) of hills and forests. No wonder the round trip took three months.

Luther wasn't interested in the treasures of Rome; the art and architecture held no fascination for him. The piers for the new St. Peter's Basilica had just been laid, but work had ceased due to lack of funds. Luther was interested only in the Rome of the saints, the Rome of relics and sacraments—he was there to pursue the path of salvation.

During his month there, he spent every moment he could celebrating mass at important shrines, visiting the catacombs, and venerating the holy relics. He was appalled by the lax moral and spiritual condition of the priests in Rome. They could rattle through six or seven masses when he had said only one. Some of them sarcastically spoke to the elements, "Bread art thou and bread thou wilt remain, and wine art thou and wine thou wilt remain."[7]

This did not invalidate the mass, however. As we have already learned, the church taught that the efficacy of the sacrament was not dependent on the lifestyle of the priests. In earlier centuries, the fear arose that some priests might be immoral and yet conduct mass. People complained that they couldn't be sure of the validity of the sacraments since they could not infallibly know the character of the priest. But the church assured them that the mass had inherent value independent of the priest's conduct.

Luther climbed the Scala Sancta (Holy Stairs), believed by the faithful to be the stairs of Pilate's judgment hall in Jerusalem. He repeated a *Pater Noster* for each one and kissed each step in the hope of delivering

Visitors to the Scala Sancta today are asked to climb the stairs only on their knees as an act of devotion. They are also assured that time will be deducted from their punishment in purgatory.

his soul from purgatory. When he got to the top of the stairs he asked, "Who knows whether it be so?"

He was not the only visitor to Rome who found the city to be filled with lax morals and widespread depravity. Erasmus of Rotterdam, who had journeyed to Rome five years earlier, wrote, "With my own ears I heard the most loathsome blasphemies against Christ and His apostles."[8]

Ignatius of Loyola, founder of the Jesuit order, refused to go to Rome because of its stupendous depravity. Pope Hadrian VI affirmed that the curia was "the origin of all evil."[9] Clearly, there was no salvation to be had in Rome.

Luther returned to the Erfurt cloister no closer to finding peace than before. If there was no salvation to be found in Rome, he did not know where to turn. He said he had gone to Rome with onions and returned with garlic.

His days in the monastery would soon be over, and he would relocate to a fledgling university to teach philosophy in a small town. And through his study of the Bible, he would eventually find the assurance of salvation he so desperately sought.

The darkness would dissipate, and light would break into his troubled soul.

5

The Great Discovery

How perfect do you have to be to get to heaven? That's the question that plagued Martin Luther. His conscience constantly reminded him that he was failing to attain the perfection he knew God demanded. Despite all of his efforts, he lacked the settled assurance that he had met even the barest minimum of God's requirements. He was a tormented soul, unsure of where to turn.

The sacraments were of some solace to him. He was taught that they were performed in order to grant grace to the penitent, and as grace was accumulated, salvation could be attained. And whatever shortcomings one might have, a "treasury of merit" won by the good deeds of other, more perfect saints, was available. Visiting relics, paying a gift, and so on could access this treasury and add to one's "account."

Luther often paid tribute to his confessor, Johann Staupitz, who patiently listened to his questions and gave him hope when he despaired of salvation. Luther confessed his sins frequently—for up to six hours on at least one occasion. He searched his soul and ransacked his memory to make sure that no sin was left unconfessed. Staupitz was so exasperated with Luther's endless confession that on one occasion he said, "If you expect Christ to forgive you, come in with something to forgive—parricide, blasphemy, adultery—instead of all these peccadilloes."[1]

But, as Roland Bainton points out, "Luther's question was not whether his sins were big or little, but whether they had been confessed."[2] He knew that God was holy and that even the smallest, single sin would be more than enough to banish him from God forever. Furthermore, he knew he couldn't trust his memory and that he may have done or thought something he didn't even realize was sinful. Even if he did remember and confess all of his sins, tomorrow would be another day. No wonder panic invaded Luther's spirit.

Here was the impasse. "Sins to be forgiven must be confessed. To be confessed they must be recognized and remembered. If they are not recognized and remembered, they cannot be confessed. If they are not confessed, they cannot be forgiven."[3] What is more, he realized that his whole nature was corrupt. We might say that confession is like mopping up a floor while the faucet is still running.

Staupitz instructed Luther to simply love God. But how could he love the God he dreaded? How could anyone love a God who is described as a "consuming fire"? How could he love a God who judged sinners and damned them to hell? In prayer, he was beset by doubts; in his study, he was beset by distractions. He selected twenty-one patron saints to pray to (three per day), all to no avail. "Love God?" he asked. And then he answered, "I hate Him."

Strong words, but Luther was desperate. He was obsessed with the image of Christ as a judge; he simply could not envision Christ as a redeemer. Staupitz refused to yield to Luther's despair and continued to provide both the counsel and hope Luther needed. "If it had not been for Dr. Staupitz," Luther said, "I should have sunk into hell."

Welcome to Wittenberg

Staupitz suggested that Luther become a professor in the town of Wittenberg, about a hundred miles from Erfurt, where a new university was being constructed under the direction of the Elector of Saxony, Prince Frederick. So it was that in 1511 Martin Luther was appointed as a teacher of philosophy. He taught the ethics of Aristotle using a commentary written by the great Catholic scholar Thomas Aquinas. Luther

Also called Frederick the Wise, Frederick III was an early defender of Luther.

complained greatly about Aristotle and, for that matter, about Aquinas. Luther was disgusted with this "man-centered" understanding of morality and ethics.

Luther concluded that Aquinas's synthesis between Christianity and Aristotle was exactly how the church became works-centered, losing sight of the true depraved nature of humanity and the need of God's grace. He was thus convinced that Aquinas, who was revered as "the teacher" in Catholic theology, had led the church astray.

Staupitz continued to advise Luther after his move to Wittenberg. He told Luther that he might be helped in his struggle toward salvation if he were to teach the Bible rather than philosophy. Luther replied that it would be so much work that "it will be the death of me!" Staupitz replied, "Quite all right. God has plenty of work for clever men to do in heaven."[4]

As it turned out, the decision to teach the Bible would be the death of Luther in a different way: he would have to die to his own efforts and accept the undeserved merit of God. In the Bible, he would find the answer his soul longed for. Clearly, Luther relished the study of the Bible. Later Staupitz, who himself held the chair of Bible at the university, would step down so that Luther could take his place.

The Matter of Salvation

In August of 1513, Luther began expounding the Psalms. When he came to Psalm 22—"My God, my God, why hast Thou forsaken me?" (KJV)— he was comforted by the fact that Christ Himself had been deserted by God. This must have been worse than the scourging, the thorns, and the nails. Thus, in Christ, Luther found someone who was overcome by a sense of alienation from God, *Anfechtungen*. Christ, Luther realized, must have experienced this because He bore our iniquity. And what he was about to learn was that the wrath of God and the love of God were brought together—both attributes were fully satisfied by the cross.

When Luther began to teach the book of Romans, he trembled at the phrase "the righteousness of God" (Rom. 1:17). Though he says he was an "impeccable monk," he stood before God as a sinner troubled in conscience. The righteousness of God struck fear into his heart because he knew that it was because of God's unbendable righteousness that sinners were cast away from His most holy presence.

Then the light dawned.

He pondered day and night the connection between the righteousness of God and the justice of God, and the statement "the just shall live by faith." Other passages also came to mind: "And to the one who does not work but believes in him who justifies the ungodly, his faith is counted as righteousness" (Rom. 4:5).

Finally he saw the connection between the justice of God and the statement "the just shall live by faith." He writes, "Then I grasped that the justice of God is that righteousness by which through grace and sheer mercy God justifies us through faith. Thereupon I felt myself to

Luther preaching in Wittenberg

be reborn and to have gone through open doors into paradise."[5]

He now understood that the "righteousness of God" not only refers to an attribute of God, but it could also be a gift from God to sinners. He no longer feared the justice of God; rather than hating God's justice, it now became inexplicably sweet. God opens His heart to those who have true faith in Christ as Savior, and Christ's holiness meets the demands of the law for us. Luther realized that we are saved by sheer grace and mercy thanks to the gift of the perfections of Christ. In the gospel we learn that sinners can be declared to have the righteousness of God attributed to their accounts. For those who believe, God has granted forgiveness and has put legions of demons to flight.

No wonder Luther objected to indulgences and would later repudiate prayers to the saints and the doctrine of purgatory. He now understood that there was a radical difference between what he had been taught as a monk and what he had learned while studying the Scriptures for himself. He had come to the assurance of saving faith based on the promises of God found in the Word of God.

When Luther was confessing his sins during his stay in the monastery, he had no assurance of salvation, for confession could at best take away only past sins, but tomorrow was another day. When he came to understand the gospel, he realized that Jesus made a perfect payment for all of his sins and that if he received that gift, he would be declared righteous until the day of his death. Yes, of course, he would continue to confess his sins to maintain his personal fellowship with God, but he now had the assurance that as God's child the righteousness of God was a permanent gift. His relationship with God was on a sure footing.

Years later, in his commentary on the book of Galatians, Luther wrote that the righteousness we receive from God is different from all other kinds of righteousness; "the righteousness of God," he says is, "a passive righteousness" given to us freely by God. Just as the earth cannot produce rain but receives it as a gift from God, even so, we do nothing to deserve the righteousness of God but receive it by faith. Righteousness based on works and the righteousness given to us by God should never be confused or mixed. Our conscience has no remedy when we are tormented by our own imperfections and sins, but we find peace when we rest in the forgiveness given to us, the righteousness of God received freely by faith.

To a friend who was weary of trying to establish his own goodness before God, Luther wrote, "Learn Christ and him crucified. Learn to pray to him and . . . say, 'Thou Lord Jesus, art my righteousness, but I am thy sin. Thou hast taken upon thyself what is mine and hast given to me what is thine. Thou hast taken upon thyself what thou wast not and hast given to me what I was not.'"[6] Luther was saying, in other words, that Christ got what He didn't deserve, namely our sin, and we got what we didn't deserve, namely His righteousness. This exchange is the heart of the gospel (2 Cor. 5:19). Luther said that we must preach this gospel to ourselves every day.

Salvation, Luther discovered, lies outside ourselves; we are justified by God's legal proclamation made in heaven; we remain sinners but are wholly accepted by God on the basis of the merit of Christ; hence, we are simultaneously *saints* and *sinners*. When Luther began to teach and preach this doctrine, it was received by many, but it also elicited the antagonism of the official church.

And so it was that the man who became known for his *Ninety-Five Theses* now entered into an arena of conflict, struggle, and unsought fame. He soon attracted the attention of the papacy and elicited both the praise of the German people and the hatred of the religious hierarchy. He could not simply retreat back into his role as a scholar in Wittenberg. He would now be on stage with the most powerful political and religious leaders of Europe.

Meanwhile in Rome

Back in Rome, Pope Leo hadn't forgotten about Luther's *Ninety-Five Theses* and decided that it was time to extinguish the furor that was happening in Germany. Luther would later say that if the pope had only silenced Johann Tetzel, who was peddling indulgences, he (Luther) would have been satisfied, and the Reformation would have gone no further. However, rather than silencing Tetzel, the pope gave him a doctorate in theology so that he'd appear to be on equal academic ground with Luther and could write his own defense of indulgences!

Clearly, Luther was underestimated. Some reformers, notably Girolamo Savonarola in Italy and John Hus in Prague, primarily attacked the morals of the church, whereas Luther went directly to what he saw as the source of the corruption—the Catholic Church's doctrine of salvation. Luther had been liberated when he discovered the doctrine of justification by faith alone, and soon thousands of others would have a similar experience of spiritual freedom. Neither the pope nor Tetzel could stop the movement.

As his theology developed, the immediate question Luther would have to settle in his mind was if the Bible alone was an infallible guide for matters of faith and practice. The conflicts that were on the horizon would force him to the conclusion that it was. And with this single conviction, Luther would challenge the traditions of the church that had evolved for centuries. The book that enabled him to understand the gospel was the book that would enable him to defend it.

Luther initially tried to stay out of the fray but kept being caught in the swirl of publicity that surrounded him. He was surprised by it all and later said he was "led like a horse with blinders on."[7] In a matter of months, Martin Luther was famous throughout Germany and was both loved and hated. He couldn't help but play a decisive role in the controversy he had so innocently begun.

Three Critical Debates

Within one year of the posting of the *Ninety-Five Theses*, Luther was invited to two debates with Catholic theologians who intended to indict him for heresy. The first debate was to be held in Heidelberg, the second in Augsburg. A third debate followed a year later in Leipzig.

Heidelberg

In May of 1518, Luther was invited to Heidelberg, Germany, to defend his theology before a large and learned group of men. His prince, Frederick the Wise, insisted that under no condition should Luther go to Rome, but he thought that Heidelberg would be safe.

Luther decided to travel on foot incognito. After four days of tramping he sarcastically said, "I am properly contrite for going on foot. Since my contrition is perfect, full penance has already been done, and no indulgence is needed."[8] He had reason to fear. His enemies boasted that he would be burned within a month.

At Heidelberg, Luther defended Augustine, who, from the Scriptures, argued that even upright acts may be mortal sins in the eyes of God. If this were true, the teaching that one can be saved by good deeds, or that our good deeds can be added to the perfect merit of Christ, was false. Even more basic, he challenged the idea that humans can properly

This memorial to Martin Luther is in Heidelberg: "Martin Luther, 1483–1546, In commemoration of his stay at the Augustinian monastery and the Heidelberg Disputation of April 26, 1518. The Luther Year, 1983."

distinguish between a mortal and a venial sin. His point, which he would make clearer later in his theological pilgrimage, was that we are so bound by sin that we cannot contribute to our own salvation—God Himself must intervene to give us grace and the gift of eternal life.

In fact, "The person who believes that he can obtain grace by doing what is in him adds to his sin so that he becomes doubly guilty."[9] Basing his views on the Bible and agreeing with Augustine, he concluded that there could be no cooperative effort between humans and God in salvation but that salvation was a work of God alone in our hearts through faith. Those who hope to attain forgiveness for their sins through works obscure the grace of God.

Luther said, "The law says 'Do this!' and it is never done. Grace says, 'Believe in this man!' and immediately everything is done."[10] The more people think they have satisfied God with their good works, the more they are damned. Thus grace can be understood only against the background of man's depravity and sin.

On his way back from Heidelberg, Luther, who was given a ride on a wagon with the delegation from Nuremberg, said that he hoped that his theology would triumph over that of his scholastic opponents. He wrote to a friend that it would be impossible to reform the church "unless canon law, the decretals, scholastic theology, philosophy, and logic, as they now exist, are absolutely eradicated and other studies instituted."[11] He was encouraged that even if the older theologians didn't agree with him, he had made headway with some of the younger students.

Augsburg

Four months after the Heidelberg disputation, Luther was summoned to Augsburg to appear before Cardinal Thomas Cajetan. Luther's friend Prince Frederick was under pressure from the pope to clear his reputation and place "this child of the devil" under the jurisdiction of the church authorities, "lest future generations reproach you with having fostered the rise of a most pernicious heresy against the Church of God."[12] This time, Prince Frederick hesitated in providing Luther with safe passage, so Luther, who expected that he might be killed, said, "Now I must die. What a disgrace I shall be to my parents!"[13]

Cajetan's intention was to either reconcile Luther to the church or send him bound to Rome. He accused Luther of denying that there was a treasury filled with the excess merits of Mary and other saints that could be accessed by those who viewed relics. He also accused him of teaching the sufficiency of faith for justification and denying that the pope had the authority to dispense indulgences.

Cajetan had three interviews with Luther, all of which came down to one simple question: Would Luther recant? Luther replied that he had not come to Augsburg to do what he could have done back in Wittenberg; he had come to Augsburg, he said, to have his errors pointed out to him. When told that the pope was above Scripture, Luther retorted, "His Holiness abuses Scripture." After the third exchange, Cajetan dismissed Luther, saying he didn't want to see him again until he recanted. Luther, in turn, reported that the cardinal was no more fitted to handle this case than "an ass to play on a harp."

Luther's confessor, Johann Staupitz, who was present at the proceedings, released Luther from his vows of obedience to the Augustinian order. And Luther, with the help of friends, escaped the city at night and returned to Wittenberg.

Prince Frederick was in a difficult position. He was being pressured by the church to send Luther bound to Rome, but his famous citizen was admired by many of the German people. The theological faculty at his university had also not repudiated Luther. Yet, because Frederick was a good Catholic prince addicted to the cult of relics, he didn't want to be accused of harboring a heretic. However, at least for the moment, he refused to condemn Luther.

Leipzig

A third debate took place in July of 1519 in Leipzig. Luther was challenged to debate the highly respected theologian Johann Eck, who arrived under heavy guard. On the opening day, the entire assembly gathered in the St. Thomas Church for mass (later Johann Sebastian Bach would serve here as the choirmaster); then they transferred to the auditorium in the Castle of Leipzig.

Eck challenged Luther on the authority of the church versus the Scriptures. Luther reiterated that pontiffs can err, and that others have the right to interpret Scripture. He questioned the premise of the infallibility of the pope based on Christ's words to Peter, "Thou art Peter and upon this rock I will build my church." When studying for the debate, Luther wrote to a friend, "I do not know whether the pope is the Antichrist himself or his apostle, so wretchedly in his decrees does he corrupt and crucify Christ, that is, the truth."[14] Luther didn't believe that every pope was the antichrist; he thought that the papacy, as an institution, was the antichrist because all the popes were usurping the role and position of Christ.

Luther had not come to these conclusions easily. He had been trained to give unquestioned allegiance to the Holy Father. The thought that the pope might be the tool of the devil came only after gut-wrenching turmoil and study.

Eck asserted that the primacy of the Roman Church dated back to the first century. Luther, however, had studied his history and pointed out that in the early centuries of Christianity, bishops in Italy and elsewhere were not subject to the bishop of Rome. Indeed, the Greek bishops never accepted the authority of Rome at any time, and they were not damned.

Eck accused Luther of following the "damned" John Wycliffe, who said, "It is not necessary for salvation to believe that the Roman Church is above all others." He also accused Luther of following the "heretic" John Hus, who had taught that Christ, not Peter, was the head of the Holy Catholic Church.

Luther retorted that councils do not have the authority to establish new articles of faith. He pointed out that they have even sometimes contradicted each other. Then came the bombshell: "A simple layman armed with Scripture is to be believed above a pope or council without it. As for the pope's decretal on indulgences I say that neither the Church nor the pope can establish articles of faith. These must come from Scripture. For the sake of Scripture we should reject pope and councils."[15]

Though they went on to debate purgatory and indulgences, the exchanges always reverted back to the question of authority: Was it the Scriptures or the pope? "Are you the only one who knows anything?" Eck kept pressing Luther. When Luther said he was following his convictions and conscience, Eck told him to abandon his conscience because it erred.

While in Leipzig, Luther was given a book written by the martyr John Hus and concluded that

Johann Sebastian Bach became minister of music at St. Thomas Church two hundred years after Luther's Leipzig debate.

he agreed with Hus on major issues, such as the corrupting influence of indulgences, the need for the authority of Christ rather than the pope, and the supremacy of Scripture. He had previously denied being a Hussite, but now he openly admitted, "We are all Hussites without knowing it." He continued, "I am a Christian theologian; and I am bound, not only to assert, but to defend the truth with my blood and death. I want to believe freely and be a slave to the authority of no one, whether council, university, or pope."[16] The debate lasted eighteen days and solidified Luther's breach with the Catholic Church. He left Leipzig through a hole in the wall, where a horse was waiting for him, then rode for several hours back to Wittenberg.

Though abandoned by many of his friends, Luther was now convinced that the Scriptures alone were the supreme authority. Like a pebble thrown into a pond, Luther's conviction caused ripples that became wider as they emanated from the controversial theologian in Wittenberg.

Eck traveled to back to Rome to inform the pope that Luther admitted to being a Hussite. Although threatened with death, the monk whom the pope called a "drunken German" refused to back down.

6

The Dominoes Begin to Fall

L
ike a man who pulled a stone from a mountain and unintentionally began an avalanche, so Martin Luther, in rescuing the gospel from centuries of encrusted traditions, caused the entire structure of the medieval church to crumble.

With renewed zeal, he continued to challenge one tradition after another. He feverishly set himself to writing tracts and books that would expound the content and implications of what he believed to be a biblically rooted theology. He began to develop his ideas rapidly, not stopping to systematize his thinking but responding to the needs of the moment. And because Luther's works were often printed as soon as they were finished, he didn't have an opportunity to correct mistakes or even tweak what he had written to keep from being misunderstood. He published two books in quick succession, later followed by a third that made his break with the church irreparable.

An Appeal to the German Nobility

"The time for silence is gone, and the time for speaking has come." Those are the introductory words that Luther penned for his book *Address to the German Nobility* (published in August of 1520). As we'll discover, throughout this address Luther exposes the tyranny of the pope, whose government "agrees with the government of the apostles about as well as Lucifer with Christ, hell with heaven."[1] He unabashedly appeals to German nationalism and the resentment many Germans had toward Rome. "In name the empire belongs to us, but in reality it belongs to the Pope. . . . Just as we thought we had achieved independence, we became the slaves of the craftiest tyrants; we have the name, title, and coat of arms of the empire, but the pope has the wealth, power, courts, and the laws. Thus the pope devours the fruit and we play with the peels."[2]

He thought that since the pope had no intention of reforming the church, the temporal powers (princes and the like) should call a council and make reforms. He argued that since the magistrate is to punish evildoers, it follows that political powers should be used to reform the religious; evil priests, for example, should be punished by the secular authorities. Church and state, he said, are responsible for the correction of each other. He thought that Germany should defend itself from "these raving wolves who come dressed in sheep's clothing as if they were shepherds and rulers." Papal officials were "a crawling mass of reptiles" who were deceiving everyone.

He then spoke about three walls that were protecting the church so that its leaders could do as they pleased without being punished. Feeling secure behind these walls, the ecclesiastical powers were "free to indulge in all matter of knavery and evil. Like the walls of Jericho, these three walls (actually 'paper walls') needed to be torn down."

The first wall that protected a corrupt church is the belief that *the spiritual power is above the temporal*; this idea, Luther said, had to be dismantled. He argued his point by appealing to the priesthood of all believers: "We are all alike Christians and have baptism, faith, the Spirit, and all things alike. If a priest is killed, the land is laid under an interdict. Why not in the case of a peasant? Whence comes this great distinction between those who are called Christians?"[3]

We should be thankful, he said, for the temporal powers, for if they were not in control, evil men would live in fearful chaos. Therefore, political rulers should be free to perform their duties without restriction, but the law should also be applied to the pope, bishops, peasants, monks, and nuns. A corrupt church should not be allowed to hide behind its own canon laws, and secular powers should dismantle the hierarchy of the corrupt church that has granted itself the power to exploit those under its control.

Later on, as Luther developed the implications of the doctrine of every believer's priesthood, there was a radical change in the way people viewed work. Whereas the church had taught that only religious exercises (such as saying a prayer, giving of alms, or participation in the sacraments) were pleasing to God, Luther concluded that all work—even the most mundane—could be to the glory of God. He said, "The idea that the service to God should have only to do with a church altar, singing, reading, sacrifice, and the like is without doubt the worst trick of the

Town of Wittenberg, 1536

devil. How could the devil have led us more effectively astray than by the narrow conception that service to God takes place only in church and by the works done therein. . . . The whole world could abound with services to the Lord, not only in churches but also in the home, kitchen, workshop, field."[4] The woman who scrubs floors glorifies God not because she sings while she works but because God likes clean floors. God milks cows, but He uses the milkmaid to do it.

A second wall protecting the church was the teaching that *only the pope can interpret Scripture*. Luther called this an "outrageous, fancied fable." He attacked the papal notion that "the Holy Spirit never leaves them [the popes], no matter how ignorant and wicked they are, they become bold and decree only what they want."[5] Therefore, if the pope has become an offense to Christendom, he shouldn't be allowed to hide behind the tradition that only he can interpret Scripture; this exclusive privilege needed to be wrested from the papacy.

In a sense, Luther's first point that affirmed the priesthood of all believers had already demolished the second wall. If we are all priests, we all have a right to read the Bible and interpret it as we see fit. "Balaam's ass was wiser than the prophet himself. If God then spoke through an ass against a prophet, why should he not be able even now to speak through a righteous man against the pope?"[6] Later, Luther would translate the Bible into the German language so that it would be accessible to common men and women.

Finally, the third wall that he said should be torn down was that *only the pope could call a*

Statue of Luther in the Marktplatz in Wittenberg

council. Luther quoted Matthew 18:16, where it speaks about reconciliation and unresolved disputes being brought "to the church." This suggests that it is not the exclusive right of the pope to call a council; the church body has an equal right to do so. He also stated that the pope should return to simplicity, with no more triple crowns, toe-kissing, and the like. He also believed that the clergy should be allowed to marry. Simply put, Luther shamed the pope by comparing him with Christ.

The *Address to the German Nobility* ended with a list of twenty-seven matters that needed reform and a challenge to the secular powers to clean up the abuses of the church. Masses for the dead should be abolished because they had become a way of getting money and thus "excited the anger of God." Public festivals (except Sunday) should be abolished since the holy days had become very "unholy." Monasteries should be reduced in number and converted into schools, with monks free to come and go at will. And the interdict (the power of the pope to decree that all sacraments in a region be withheld) should be abolished since it silenced God's Word and was "a greater sin than killing twenty Popes at once." And after listing other necessary reforms, he concluded by saying, "May God grant us all a Christian understanding, and especially to the Christian nobility of the German nation true spiritual courage, to do what is best for our unhappy Church. Amen."[7]

The Aftermath

The German people welcomed this grandiose proposal, which was originally intended to be just a tract. But the tract grew into a book of ninety-six pages and sold four thousand copies in two weeks—a huge number in those days. The idea that the secular powers could exercise authority over corrupt religious leaders appealed to the frustrated Germans, who felt helpless in the face of the controlling demands of the papacy and an exalted, corrupt, and protected priesthood.

No doubt Luther felt personally indebted to the temporal powers of the state. After all, it was because of his prince's political power that Luther's life had been protected. But by putting the state on equal footing with the ecclesiastical powers, he encouraged the political rulers to weigh in on his reforms.

We wish we could say that the Reformation Luther began was just a spiritual movement and that Luther preached the gospel, people listened and were converted, and the shackles of the church were cast off. But as historian Phillip Schaff notes, "Violent passions, political intrigues, the ambition and avarice of princes, and all sorts of selfish and worldly motives were mixed up with the war against the papacy."[8] Luther wanted to keep the Reformation primarily a spiritual revolt against the church, but his appeal to German nationalism would play a large part in the reforms he sought.

Ideas have consequences. His *Address*, which is just one of several political writings he penned, would have long-term implications for Germany and the world. As we shall see in a later chapter, there are those who believe that Luther's teachings on church/state issues contributed to the nationalism of Germany and the strict, militaristic obedience of soldiers during the terrible atrocities of World War II. Some would say that by putting a great emphasis on the divine source of temporal authority, Luther's teaching led to an unqualified endorsement of "state power."

Indeed, Luther himself would soon discover the consequences of his own writings during a peasant revolt in Germany. His controversial response would reverberate for centuries to come. We shall have to return to this important subject in a later chapter.

When he neared the end of the *Address*, he said that he had "another song to sing and he will sing it with all of his might." He had in mind another book, one that would attack the sacramental system of the church that held people bound.

The Babylonian Captivity of the Church

In his most radical book, *The Babylonian Captivity of the Church*, Martin Luther set out to show that the sacraments were not the exclusive channels of grace as administered by the clergy.

At the beginning of the book, he says that there are really only three sacraments: baptism, the Lord's Supper, and, in a secondary sense, confession. But near the end of the treatise he affirms only two: baptism and the Lord's Supper. As for confession, he thought that though it should be practiced, it should not be viewed as a sacrament. Since baptism and the Lord's Supper were the only two instituted by Christ, the church should not go beyond what He had prescribed. By now Luther understood more clearly that salvation was attained by faith in what Christ had accomplished on the cross, not through submission to the rites of the church.

The title for *The Babylonian Captivity of the Church* was derived from the experience of the Jews in the Old Testament when they were held as captives in Babylon for seventy years. In Luther's view, the pope actually chained people to the church as captives by using the sacraments to control the populace and withhold salvation from whomever the priests wished. Hence, the people were in perpetual slavery.

Reviewing the Sacramental System

We must remember that early in the history of the church, salvation was, in some way, connected to the sacraments of baptism and the Lord's Supper. For example, Ignatius of Antioch (c. AD 115) wrote that "the Eucharist is the flesh of our Savior, Jesus Christ, who suffered for our sins and who the Father, in His goodness, raised up again." By eating and drinking we become partakers of eternal life.[9] In the so-called *Second Letter of Clement* (author unknown), eternal life is spoken of as being granted at baptism. This was the origin of the belief that salvation came through the sacraments of the Lord's Supper and baptism. As a result, infants were baptized, and particularly in North Africa, they were also given the bread and wine. After all, if the sacraments grant grace, why should children be denied the grace that comes though *both* baptism and the Lord's Supper?

After the time of Constantine (fourth century), sacramentalism (the teaching that the sacraments are the means by which grace is infused into the soul) shifted into high gear. From then on, the church would at times be used for political purposes, and the sacraments would often be the means by which the church could control the lives of those who lived in the Roman Empire. As sacramentalism grew, so did the liturgy that accompanied it. Hence Voltaire's remark that the mass is the "grand opera of the poor."

As the centuries progressed, seven sacraments were identified. Space forbids a detailed exposition of each one, but the basic teaching was that each sacrament dispensed grace; however, no one sacrament dispensed enough grace to save a sinner. Assurance of salvation was beyond reach because no one could be assured that they had enough grace to gain admittance into heaven.

And what if the priest who administered the sacraments wasn't living a holy life? In a previous chapter we quoted Augustine, who said that sacraments have inherent power (*ex opere operato*) even if they are administered by thieves and robbers. This was necessary to preserve the validity of the sacraments.

In recent years, many priests in the United States and Europe have been found guilty of child sexual abuse. Never once did we hear a report suggesting that the sacraments they conducted were invalid. By disconnecting the lifestyle of the priest from the inherent value of the sacraments, the church freed itself from the fear that the sacraments would be invalidated by a criminal priest.

Think this through: if the lifestyle of the priest is unrelated to the efficacy of the sacraments, what about the lifestyle of the parishioner who receives the mass? The church answered that as long as the recipient had no mortal sin on his or her conscience, he or she can also benefit from the sacraments—even without a change of heart—though, of course, people were encouraged to have "a good inner motive." Repentance was not necessary to benefit from the sacrament.

Furthermore, as the centuries went by, the church also taught the doctrine of transubstantiation: that the priest has the power to take ordinary bread and wine and turn it into the literal body and blood of Christ. A handbook for priests published in 1927 taught that when the priests pronounce the word of consecration,

> the Incarnate Word has obliged Himself to obey and to come into their hands under the sacramental [appearance of bread and wine]. . . . God Himself descends on the altar, that He comes whenever they call Him, and as often as they call Him . . . : they may, if they wish, shut Him up in the tabernacle, or expose Him on the altar, or carry Him outside the church; they may, if they choose, eat His flesh, and give Him for the food of others.[10]

This explains why, in a Catholic church, the faithful genuflect in front of the tabernacle where the consecrated bread and wine are stored. They believe that the elements are God in His entirety. In 1546, the Council of Trent codified Roman Catholic teaching and said that the highest form of worship—worship worthy of God Himself—may be rendered to these transformed elements. To quote, the faithful may "render in veneration the worship of latria, which is due the true God, to this most holy sacrament."[11]

Luther's Critique

In *The Babylonian Captivity of the Church*, Martin Luther argues against the notion that the sacraments have inherent value without faith and a repentant heart. As Roland Bainton puts it, "This insistence upon faith diminished the role of the priests who may place a wafer in the mouth but cannot engender faith in the heart."[12] In fact, as we have already learned, Luther affirms that we are all priests before God. By saying this, he threatened the very heart of Catholic worship. He stood against a thousand years of church teaching by removing the great gulf that had developed between clergy and laity.

Luther continued to believe in the mass, but he disagreed with transubstantiation. For Luther, Christ was "literally present," but the bread remained bread, and the wine remained wine. He also taught that Christ is not sacrificed again in the mass because His sacrifice was made once and for all on the cross. Also, in Roman Catholic practice only the priests drank the wine at the mass because they feared that the laity, in clumsiness, might spill some of the blood of God. Luther felt reverence for the sacrament but insisted that the cup should be given to all believers.

The bottom line is that Luther attacked the idea that a priest had the power to "make God" and sacrifice Christ on the altar. God was present in the elements, but their value to us depended on a proper attitude of heart. "The mass is a divine promise which can help no one, be applied for no one, intercede for no one, and be communicated to none save him only who believes with a faith of his own."[13]

In the Catholic tradition of the time, the ordination of priests was also a sacrament, a ritual that elevated them above the common people. Luther maintained that such an act simply recognized the freedom of the minister to perform the duties of his office, but it didn't give him a higher character or make him exempt from the jurisdiction of the civil courts; nor did this give him a special right to perform the sacraments unless it was understood that every Christian had such a right. Gone was the tradition of an exalted priesthood. Ordination vows, Luther said, do not give the priests magical powers to dispense salvation.

In fact, as far as Luther was concerned, ordination as practiced resulted in a "detestable tyranny" of the clergy over the laity. Their

A Catholic priest performing the Tridentine Mass (Roman Rite Mass celebrated in Latin) in the twenty-first century

vestments and rituals were used to intimidate the common worshipers, causing them to think that their salvation rested in the hands of men who were separated from them as far as heaven is from the earth. The priest recited the liturgy of the mass in a dead language that the people didn't comprehend, and the church said that it wasn't necessary for them to understand what was being said since the mass had inherent power.

As for baptism, Luther retained the view that the ritual washes away original sin. He wrote, "The first point is the divine promise" and "Our entire salvation depends on this. . . . [By remembering their baptism Christians found their faith] constantly aroused and cultivated. Once the divine promise has been accepted by us, its truth lasts until death. . . . If God is for me, who can be against me?"[14]

Luther tried his best to connect infant baptism with faith. On one level he argued that a child might have unconscious faith, just as a man has faith while sleeping. Elsewhere he says that the parents have faith on behalf of the child and believe for the child vicariously. At any rate, baptism did not have power *ex opere operato*; it had to be connected with the promises of God. There is no necessary connection between baptism and conversion; without faith, one cannot be saved.

Despite being unable to link infant baptism with faith, Luther still believed that the sacrament of baptism should be administered to all infants regardless of the personal piety of the parents. Baptism therefore retained the tie between church and state; infant baptism was a "sociological sacrament" that united everyone to the wider state church. Yet he also believed that salvation was ultimately an individual matter received through faith in Christ. I personally believe that this tension between a regional church (all who are baptized) and the true church (all who are saved through faith) was never resolved in his theology. (And for that matter, I believe it cannot be resolved on the basis of the New Testament.)

Nevertheless, Luther struck a chord with the German people. From now on there would be three fundamental doctrines that would guide Luther and other reformers: "The supremacy of the *Scriptures* over tradition, the supremacy of *faith* over works, and the supremacy of the Christian *people* over an exclusive priesthood."[15]

No wonder when Erasmus read *The Babylonian Captivity of the Church* he remarked, "The breach is irreparable." Luther could only move forward and face the building opposition. In contemporary terms, the genie was out of the bottle. Now that the very structure of medieval Catholicism had been exposed and found to be wanting, Luther's ideas could never be pushed back into the ecclesiastical bottle again. Official Christendom would attempt to persecute Luther and his heretical followers, but they could never squelch the ideas that extended salvation to everyone in response to individual faith without the obstructions of the church.

Once the people were liberated from the binding chains of the church, even the persecution of these "heretics" was only moderately successful. Many who tasted the freedom of a direct relationship with God through Christ refused to back down.

As for Luther, many challenges awaited him. Pope Leo believed the time had come for some stronger measures against this "heretic," and Luther would have to respond. Five centuries later, we still admire Luther's courage and determination. Pope Leo underestimated the stamina and resolve of the "heretics" within his vast domain.

Luther was a flawed man, but a coward he was not.

7

The Wild Boar
in the Vineyard of the Lord

P ope Leo may have called Martin Luther a "drunken German who will think differently when he is sober," but although Luther enjoyed drinking beer, he was not a drunk, and he adamantly refused to think differently, come what may. He had written books that undercut the authority of the sacraments and the priests, and hence the authority of the pope. His books were widely read and discussed in Germany, and, most critically for the church, his views were gaining momentum.

The pope concluded it was time for stronger measures. A papal bull dated June 15, 1520, was sent to Luther, complete with the insignia of the pope himself. It begins with the now famous words, "Arise, O Lord, and judge thy cause. A wild boar has invaded thy vineyard. Arise, O Peter, and consider the case of the Holy Roman Church, the mother of all churches, consecrated by thy blood. Arise, O Paul."

This bull is known historically by the first two words of the Latin version, *Exsurge Domine* ("Arise O Lord"), and reiterated the grief that Luther had caused the church. "We can no longer suffer the serpent to creep through the field of the Lord. The books of Martin Luther which contain these errors are to be examined and burned."[1] The document listed forty-one "errors" from Luther's *Ninety-Five Theses*, and he was expected to recant all of them.

The errors included such matters as his objection to the view that the sacraments in and of themselves had the power of saving grace, and his rejection of indulgences and purgatory. Luther also erred because he rejected the tradition that the pope was the vicar of Christ and therefore could establish articles of faith. The bull ends with this appeal: "Now therefore we give Martin sixty days in which to submit, dating from the time of the publication of this bull in his district. Anyone who presumes to infringe our excommunication and anathema will stand under the wrath of Almighty God and the apostles Peter and Paul."[2]

A few weeks after the bull was authorized, the pope wrote a letter to Luther's friend, Prince Frederick. The letter alerted the prince that the bull that listed Luther's errors had been sealed with lead and sent. The pope wanted the prince to know that Luther "seduces the simple, and relaxes the bonds of obedience, continence, and humility." The letter ends with this admonition: "We exhort you to induce him to return to sanity and receive our clemency. If he persists in his madness, take

The full title of this papal bull is "Bull against the errors of Martin Luther and his followers."

him captive."[3] Pope Leo's letter also mentioned that the bull was being published throughout the empire and that the sixty-day grace period for Luther would begin when the bull officially arrived in Wittenberg.

Frederick—bless him—once again found himself in a difficult position. He was a loyal Catholic and felt an obligation to obey papal directives; on the other hand, his famous citizen was popular in Germany, and what is more, many of the faculty in the University of Wittenberg agreed with Luther and yet were not being accused of heresy. Frederick didn't defend Luther's theology, but he did insist that Luther be given a proper hearing. So the prince declined to act and chose to wait and see how events would unfold.

The bull would not reach Luther for three months. Through word of mouth, he knew it was on its way and what was in it. His mood vacillated between anger and even rage, saying at one point that he advocated violence: "If we punish heretics with fire, why do we not rather assault these monsters of perdition, these cardinals, these popes, and the whole swarm of the Roman Sodom, who corrupt youth and the Church of God? Why do we not rather assault them with arms and wash our hands in their blood?"[4] He retracted his strong words, saying he didn't really mean what his statement implied, and it is true that Luther did not advocate the killing of heretics. However, these words would later be held against him at the Diet of Worms.

Luther's more thoughtful response was written to a fellow minister: "Our warfare is not with flesh and blood, but against spiritual wickedness in the heavenly places, against the world rulers of this darkness. Let us then stand firm and heed the trumpet of the Lord. Satan is fighting, not against us, but against Christ in us."[5]

In response to the bull, which he had not yet seen, Luther wrote a treatise called *Against the Execrable Bull of Antichrist*. His tone was combative: "I ask thee, ignorant Antichrist, dost thou think that with thy naked words thou canst prevail against the armor of Scripture?"

He then calls his enemies by various names and concludes, "It is better that I should die a thousand times than that I should retract one syllable of the condemned articles. And as they excommunicated me for the sacrilege of heresy, so I excommunicate them in the name of the sacred truth of God. Christ will judge whose excommunication will stand. Amen."[6]

Luther was in no mood to compromise.

An Appeal to the Pope

Luther was an irrepressible man by any account. With the bull that condemned him still on its way to Wittenberg, he decided to write a book to appeal to the pope. Surprisingly, it doesn't have the combative tone we have come to expect from Luther; indeed, it's somewhat subdued, even at times honoring the pope, but there's always the appeal for the pope to understand Luther's cause.

The Freedom of a Christian is Luther's most deferential treatise, as he attempts to reason with the pope about the need to clean up the corruption in the church. He even professes great respect and honor for the pontiff. Luther tells Pope Leo that he simply might not realize that those who surround him are corrupt. He writes, "So I come, most blessed father, and, prostrate before you, pray that if possible you intervene and stop those . . . who are the enemies of peace while they pretend to keep peace."[7] Luther blames the pope's misconceptions of him on Johann Eck, who he said was responsible for the evils that surround the "Holy Father."

However, as the book progresses it's clear that the distinction he makes at the beginning between the goodness of the pope and the evil of the Roman curia quickly collapses, and the pope is implicated in the evils of the church. How else can we interpret his words, "I have truly despised your see, the Roman Curia, which, however, neither you nor anyone else can deny is more corrupt than any Babylon or Sodom ever was, and which, as far as I can see, is characterized by a completely depraved, hopeless, and notorious godlessness."[8]

And yet Luther goes on to give wise insights into the nature of Christian liberty. He discusses these questions: What is freedom for the Christian? What is the relationship between discipline and servitude for Christ? Luther writes two important statements that appear to be contradictory but must be held in tension: "A Christian is a perfectly free lord of all, subject to none. A Christian is a perfectly dutiful servant of all, subject to all."[9]

He argues that although these statements appear to be in opposition, they are both found in the writings of Paul (1 Cor. 9:19). By the first statement he's referring to liberty according to the gospel—that there is liberty *in* Christ but not *from* Christ. To put it differently, the Christian is lord of all and subject to none by virtue of faith; he is servant of all by virtue of love. "By faith we are caught up beyond ourselves into God. By love we descend beneath ourselves to our neighbor."[10] In Luther's words, "From faith thus flow forth love and joy in the Lord, and from love a joyful, willing, and free mind that serves one's neighbor willingly and takes no account of gratitude or ingratitude, of praise or blame, of gain or loss."[11]

The Christian ought to think, "Although I am an unworthy and condemned man, my God has given me in Christ all the riches of righteousness and salvation without any merit on my part. . . . Why should I not therefore freely, joyfully, with all my heart, and with an eager will do all things which I know are pleasing and acceptable to such a Father who has overwhelmed me with his inestimable riches? I will therefore give myself as a Christ to my neighbor, just as Christ offered himself to me."[12] The sequence here is important. It is from faith that love flows so that one can serve his or her neighbor—no matter the cost—whether the service ends in gain or loss. Put simply, works are not the means of salvation; they are the fruit of salvation.

Earlier in his sermon on good works, he made the point that without faith works are "idle, damnable sins." No human righteousness can be acceptable to God without the mediation of Christ. We must preach law and gospel; the law shows us what sin is that we might believe; then having believed, we do what is good. Good works do not make a person good, but a good person will do good works.

We do not know whether Pope Leo ever read Luther's book, even though it was dedicated to him. It is doubtful that the pope would have had the humility to read what this "heretic" had to say, even if it was written in a thoughtful, conciliatory tone. And as for Luther, it didn't take long for him to revert to his vitriolic, bombastic, and sarcastic diatribe against the pope and the bull, which would eventually reach Wittenberg.

The Papal Bull Arrives in Wittenberg

Luther dated *The Freedom of a Christian* on September 6, 1520. Just over a month later, on October 10, the papal bull arrived in Wittenberg. Luther could now read it for himself. He commented to Spalatin, "This bull condemns Christ himself. It summons me not to an audience but to a recantation. . . . I rejoice to suffer in so noble a cause. I am not worthy of so holy a trial. I feel much freer now that I am certain the pope is Antichrist."[13]

Luther was not in a conciliatory mood. For example, out of the forty-one charges brought against him in the bull, he chose to respond to charge 18, which accused him of saying that "indulgences were 'the pious defrauding of the faithful.'" To this, Luther sarcastically "recants" saying, "I was wrong, I admit it, when I said that indulgences were 'the pious defrauding of the faithful.' I recant and I say, 'Indulgences are the most impious frauds and imposters of the most rascally pontiffs, by which they deceive the souls and destroy the goods of the faithful.'"[14]

The marketplace in Wittenberg, where Luther received the papal bull. Luther later burned the bull in a special ceremony at the Elster Gate leading into the city.

Or consider Luther's response to charge 29, which accused him of saying that "certain articles of John Hus are most Christian, true, and evangelical, which the universal church cannot condemn." Luther replies, "I was wrong. I retract the statement that certain articles of John Hus are evangelical. I say now, 'Not some but *all* the articles of John Hus were condemned by Antichrist and his apostles in the synagogue of Satan.'"[15] Hus was burned, and so Luther prepared himself for the same fate.

Many who were loyal to the ecclesiastical powers saw to it that Luther's books were burned in cities like Cologne and Erfurt. But Luther was winning the hearts of the populace. Proof of this is found when Eck, the pope's emissary, brought a copy of the bull to Leipzig. Eck was met with such opposition that he ran and hid in fear!

The Burning of the Bull

Since Luther's books were being burned in some cities, Wittenberg decided to reply in kind. They would burn the papal bull and the decretals (canon law) of the church to show their defiance of the pope. Counting from the day the bull finally reached Wittenberg, the sixty days given Luther to recant expired on December 10, 1520. An invitation on a bulletin board read as follows.

> All friends of evangelical truth are invited to assemble, about nine o'clock, at the church of the Holy Cross, beyond the city wall. There, according to ancient, apostolic usage, the godless books of the papal constitutions and the scholastic theology will be burned, inasmuch as the presumption of the enemies of the Gospel has advanced to such a degree that they have cast the godly, evangelical books of Luther into the fire. Let all earnest students, therefore, appear at the spectacle; for it is now the time when Antichrist must be exposed.[16]

Luther was present at the burning, throwing the anti-Christian decretals into the fire along with the bull of Pope Leo X. He said, "Because you have grieved the saints of the Lord, may eternal fire grieve you."[17] And with that, he returned to town along with many of the teachers

When Luther burned the papal bull, he passed the point of no return.

and some students while others stayed and sang around the fire. For Luther, this meant that the final judgment of the pope (the antichrist) was about to begin.

After dinner, the celebration continued with students riding on a farmer's wagon and a flagbearer holding a long pole with a supposed "papal bull," four feet long, held high in the wind. Also on the wagon was a trumpet player who called attention to what was happening. Many people were delighted with the procession and applauded. That evening, the burning of the bull was again reenacted with much laughter and gaiety. Luther was not present for these pranks, but the next day he told the students, "Unless you contradict with your whole heart the ridiculous rule of the pope, you shall not be saved. For the kingdom of the pope is so contrary to the kingdom of Christ and to Christian life that it would be better and safer to live all alone in the desert than to live in the kingdom of Antichrist."[18]

Luther would later say that he was excommunicated three times: when his confessor Staupitz released him from his vow of obedience to the order; when the pope cut him off from his church; and finally, when the emperor cut him off from his empire (to be described in the next chapter). This triple excommunication was painful but necessary so that he could freely expose the errors of the church. He found comfort in Psalm 27:10 "When my father and mother forsake me, then the LORD will take me up" (KJV).

Luther had defied the pope, and "the wild boar" continued to destroy "the vineyard of the Lord." And whether Pope Leo was happy about it—and he was not—the "vineyard of the Lord" would never be the same again.

8

Here I Stand

Pope Leo X ignored Martin Luther's request for a hearing, so Luther appealed to Charles V, the newly crowned emperor. Luther wrote to him saying that it was not unseemly that he, a peasant, should approach an earthly prince, nor was it unseemly that an earthly prince should stoop to raise the poor from the dust.

In his *Address to the German Nobility*, Luther argued that it was not the prerogative of the pope alone to call a council. He challenged secular powers to take matters into their own hands to dismantle the church's hierarchy with its unwarranted authority and obvious corruption. Charles, Luther said, could call a council.

In other words, Luther appealed his case to Caesar. He had already put forth specific ways by which the church could be reformed so that it could return to spiritual simplicity and the gospel that motivated the early apostles. Christ washed the disciples' feet, Luther remarked, whereas the pope required that his toe be kissed.

Needless to say, the papacy was strongly opposed to the notion that the secular powers should preside over a council. After all, the spiritual

Holy Roman Emperor Charles V endorsed both the Council of Trent and the Order of the Jesuits as ways to combat Protestantism.

powers were above the secular, so the political authorities were expected to do the will of the spiritual without too much ado—and the papacy wanted the secular powers to put Luther to death as soon as possible.

But Charles had his own concerns. He wanted to assert his own recently acquired authority, and more to the point, he knew about Luther's popularity and the fact that the church was in desperate need of at least a few reforms. To move against Luther without giving him a hearing would incur the wrath of a people whose favor he curried. Furthermore, he wanted to maintain a cordial relationship with Luther's prince, Elector Frederick.

Keep in mind that there were only seven electors in the Holy Roman Empire, and their responsibility was to elect the emperor. Frederick had voted for Charles in 1519 when the vacancy had to be filled. In fact, when Charles was crowned in Aachen, Germany, he and Elector Frederick conferred and agreed that Luther should not be condemned without a hearing. But the question was, where should such a hearing be held?

As king, Charles had inherited the domains of Austria, Spain, and the Netherlands. And now that he had been elected emperor over Germany, he ruled over more territory than any leader since Charlemagne. Charles didn't want to risk the alienation of the German population.

Most of Germany appeared to be on Luther's side. One observer said that nine-tenths of Germany was for Luther and one-tenth was shouting, "Death to the pope." So far, Elector Frederick had managed

Martin Luther in front of Charles V (1500–1558) at the Diet of Worms, April 16, 1521

to appease both the people and the pope by excusing the burning of the papal bull on the grounds that Luther's books were being burned illegally. Regardless, the pope wanted Luther dead, and Charles knew that disposing of this famous German was not quite that simple.

As a devout Catholic, Emperor Charles knew that the question of Luther could not be postponed indefinitely. After extending Luther an invitation (and rescinding it several times), the date was finally set for a hearing in Worms, Germany, in April of 1521.

The Diet of Worms

Luther expected that his trip to Worms, as with Augsburg, meant he was going to his death. He said, "My head is worth nothing compared to Christ." Then with biting sarcasm he wrote, "I believe in the pope, binder and looser in heaven, earth, and hell, and in Simony, his only son our lord, who was conceived by the canon law and born of the Romish church. Under his power truth suffered, was crucified, dead, and buried."[1]

His parody of the Apostles' Creed continues as he excoriates the pope and depicts Charles sitting on the right hand of Paul, ready to rule over worldly things. As for his response to the invitation to go to Worms, Luther was defiant. "I will reply to the emperor that if I am being invited simply to recant I will not come. If to recant is all that is wanted, I can do that perfectly well right here. But if he is inviting me to my death, then I will come. I hope none but the papists will stain their hands in my blood. Antichrist reigns. The Lord's will be done."[2] To another he wrote, "This shall be my recantation at Worms: 'Previously I said the pope is the vicar of Christ. I recant. Now I say the pope is the adversary of Christ and the apostle of the Devil.'"[3]

Soon Luther's resolve would be tested in the presence of the most powerful man in Europe and his large entourage. He would be invited to stand before the mighty of this world and prove that he believed in what he was saying and wasn't just blustering.

The Journey to Worms

Luther was assured of safe passage as he set out with horse and carriage for Worms. On April 16, he entered the city as a conquering hero. Two thousand people turned out to escort him to his lodging. Luther later said that he would have gone to Worms even if there were as many devils there as there were tiles on the rooftops.

The day after arriving, he was taken to the assembly, where he stood before German princes, dignitaries, and Emperor Charles—the heir to a long line of Catholic sovereigns and a symbol of medieval power and heritage. There he was examined by Eck, an official of the archbishop of Trier (to be distinguished from the Eck who interrogated him years earlier in Leipzig) and confronted with a pile of books.

Luther was asked whether the books were his. When he answered yes, he was asked if he was willing to defend them all. He begged for time to think it over and was granted his request.

That night, after being taken to his lodging, he prayed. Although this prayer is lengthy, I quote it here for its pathos, heartfelt anguish, and courage.

> O Almighty and Everlasting God, how terrible is this world! Behold it openeth its mouth to swallow me up, and I have so little trust in Thee. . . . How weak is the flesh, and Satan how strong! If it is only in the strength of this world that I must put my trust, all is over. . . . My last hour is come, my condemnation has been pronounced. . . . O God, O God! . . . O God, do Thou help me against all the wisdom of this world. Do this; Thou shouldest do this . . . Thou alone . . . for this is not my work, but Thine. I have nothing to do here, nothing to contend for with these great ones of the world. I should desire to see my days flow on peaceful and happy. But the cause is Thine . . . and it is a Righteous and Eternal Cause. O Lord, help me! Faithful and unchangeable God, in no man do I place my trust. It would be vain. All that is of man is uncertain; all that cometh of man fails . . . O God, my God, hearest Thou me not? . . . My God, art Thou dead? . . . No, Thou canst not die. Thou only hidest Thyself. Thou hast chosen me for this work. I know it well! . . . Act then O God . . . stand at my side, for the sake of Thy Well-Beloved Jesus Christ, Who is my Defense, my Shield, and my strong Tower.

After a moment of struggle, Luther continued,

> Lord where stayest Thou? . . . O my God, where art Thou? . . . Come, come; I am ready . . . I am ready to lay down my life for Thy Truth . . . patient as a lamb. For it is the cause of justice—it is Thine . . . I will never separate myself from Thee, neither now nor through Eternity. . . . And though the world should be filled with devils—though my body, which is still the work of Thy hands, should be slain, be stretched upon the

pavement, be cut in pieces . . . reduced to ashes . . . my soul is Thine. . . .
Yes; Thy Word is my assurance of it. My soul belongs to Thee. It shall
abide forever with Thee. . . . Amen.[4]

He awoke knowing that this would be the day he would have to answer
the question of whether he would defend his writings with a yes or a
no. He didn't realize the impact his decision would have on Germany,
Europe, and us all. It's chilling to think of how different the history of
Christianity would be if Luther had buckled under pressure.

Here I Stand

The postponement to defend his books until the next day actually
granted Luther a larger audience as the full Diet met for deliberations.
All the powerful leaders of Germany were present: Charles V along with
lords, princes, and wealthy men. Due to the numbers, a larger hall was
chosen, and even it was crowded.

Eck again showed Luther the books on the table and reiterated the
question of the previous day. Luther again answered that yes, they were
his. When asked whether he would renounce all of them, he replied
that they were not all of "one sort." Some of his books dealt with faith
and life, with which all could agree; others dealt with the issues of the
papacy, and these needed discussion. A third class of his books dealt
with attacks against specific individuals, and though he confessed that
he was more sarcastic than might have been necessary, the matters still
needed to be debated. He ended by saying that if he could be shown
that his books were contrary to Scripture, he would be the first to throw
them into the fire.

Eck replied that it was characteristic of heretics to defend their writings from Scripture. Indeed, he said that Luther was repeating the errors of Hus and Wycliffe. How could he assume that he alone was
able to interpret Scripture? Finally, the challenge was clear. "I ask you,

Another depiction of Martin Luther in front of Charles V (1500–1558) at the Diet of Worms, April 16, 1521

Martin—answer candidly and without horns—do you or do you not repudiate your books and the errors which they contain?"

Luther replied,

> Since then Your Majesty and your lordships desire a simple reply, I will answer without horns and without teeth. Unless I am convicted by Scripture and plain reason—I do not accept the authority of popes and councils, for they have contradicted each other—my conscience is captive to the Word of God. I cannot and I will not recant anything, for to go against conscience is neither right nor safe. God help me. Amen.[5]

The earliest version added the words, "Here I stand, I cannot do otherwise," though the words were not recorded on the spot. Nevertheless, they are probably genuine. As Roland Bainton suggests in his book *Here I Stand*, the scribe may have been too moved to write Luther's final declaration.[6]

Luther had spoken in German but was asked to repeat his words in Latin. He threw his hands in the air with a gesture of despair, then slipped out of the hall and went to his lodging. Meanwhile, Emperor Charles requested that Luther's words be deliberated. Those present asked for time to respond, which Charles granted. Then after giving them his own confession of faith, he added, "A single friar who goes counter to all Christianity for a thousand years must be wrong. Therefore I am resolved to stake my lands, my friends, my body, my blood, my life, and my soul. . . . He [Luther] may return under his safe conduct, but without preaching or making any tumult. I will proceed against him as a notorious heretic, and ask you to declare yourselves as you promised me."[7]

The electors were then presented with the document to sign. Six of the seven were present, but two of them, one of whom was Frederick the Wise, refused to sign. At last Frederick clearly declared himself as being on Luther's side. Nevertheless, Charles began to move against Luther who, as a heretic, could be killed without any reprisals. He had been promised safe-conduct, so the plan was to let him return home before seizing him and putting him to death.

Later, a more complete copy of the Edict of Worms accused Luther of defaming marriage and denying the body and the blood of the Lord. "He makes the sacraments depend on the faith of the recipient. He is pagan in his denial of free will. This devil in the habit of a monk has brought together ancient errors into one stinking puddle and has invented new ones. . . . His teaching makes for rebellion, division, war, murder, robbery, arson, and the collapse of Christendom." The edict ended by saying that Luther was to be regarded as a convicted heretic and that no one was to harbor him. "His followers also are to be condemned. His books are to be eradicated from the memory of man."[8]

Before Luther left Worms, further attempts were made to get him to recant by telling him that much of what he had said about the church was true and reform was needed. But if he did not recant some of his writings, then "the seamless robe of Christendom" would be rent and the church would fragment, taking society down with it. But Luther didn't buckle under the pressure and refused to recant so much as a single article of what he'd written. For this, he would spend the rest of his life as an outlaw. And yes, "the seamless robe of Christendom" would be torn in two.

An Unexpected Stay at the Wartburg Castle

Luther left Worms on April 26 and preached in various towns en route to his home. Though rumors circulated that he was dead, he was actually very much alive. On the morning of May 4, while going through the Thüringen forest, five masked riders swept down on him, lifted him from his cart, and rode off to the town of Eisenach. Thankfully, these were friends, not enemies.

Frederick the Wise had asked his riders to "capture" Luther and take him to the Wartburg Castle, whose rocky heights overlooked the beautiful town of Eisenach. With the exception of a brief visit to Wittenberg, he stayed in his castle room for ten months. It was here in isolation that Luther had one of the most productive periods of his life. Amid his doubts, depression, confusion, and insomnia, he feverishly wrote books and pamphlets, and most astoundingly of all, translated the New Testament into German in just eleven weeks.

Wartburg Castle

Luther and the Devil

The Wartburg Castle symbolized a day when German knighthood was at its height; within its walls were the relics of St. Elizabeth and other German heroes. But Luther wasn't interested in these treasures; he was overcome by the spiritual battles that his own actions and beliefs had brought on.

In his room, which served as both a study and a bedroom, he struggled with the devil's greatest weapon against the saints: doubt and conflict of soul. He kept struggling with questions such as, Are you alone wise? and Have all those in previous centuries been in error? If you are in error, you are taking so many others with you to hell. Roland Bainton writes that Luther "passed from one self-incrimination to another."[9]

Luther said, "I can tell you in this idle solitude there are a thousand battles with Satan. It is much easier to fight against the incarnate Devil—that is, against men—than against spiritual wickedness in the heavenly places. Often I fall and am lifted again by God's right hand."[10]

It is in his room in the Wartburg Castle that tradition says Luther "threw an inkwell at the devil." In fact, it's said that tour guides would rub a bit of soot on the wall near the stove so that visitors could see where the inkwell landed. However, it's doubtful that Luther literally threw an inkwell at the devil. In his *Table Talks* he said, "I fought the devil with ink!" What he meant was that he fought the devil by the translation of the Scriptures into the German language. The devil is not afraid of a flying inkwell, but he is afraid of God's Word in the hearts and minds of God's people.

In his struggles with the devil, Luther was well aware of how easily human beings can be deceived. Perhaps he was more sensitive to such deception because of the experience of St. Martin, the figure in church history for whom he was named. The story goes that St. Martin had a vision of Christ dressed in regal clothes, but when St. Martin glanced at Christ's hands to see the nail prints, the apparition disappeared. Martin never knew whether he had been visited by Christ or the devil.

Thus, Luther also wondered whether his ideas were from God or were deceptions of the evil one.

In his excellent book *Luther: Man between God and the Devil*, Heiko A. Oberman argues that we misunderstand Luther if we think that his conception of the devil can be dismissed as a medieval phenomenon. Oberman writes, "Christ and the Devil were equally real to him: one was the perpetual intercessor for Christianity, the other a menace to mankind till the end. . . . Christ and Satan wage a cosmic war for mastery over Church and world. No one can evade involvement in this struggle. . . . The Devil is the omnipresent threat, and exactly for this reason the faithful need the proper weapons for survival."[11] Luther distinguished between the superstitions of the time and the teaching of Scripture about the devil.

Encountering the devil wasn't new to Luther. He'd already faced him in the monastery in Wittenberg. The devil, he said, would come and thump about in a storage chamber behind the stove. He also heard him over the chamber in the monastery. Luther responded, "But when I realized it was Satan, I rolled over and went back to sleep again." Luther explains

Luther's study inside Wartburg Castle

that it is not as a poltergeist that the devil discloses his true nature "but as the adversary who thwarts the Word of God; only then is he really to be feared. He seeks to capture the conscience, can quote the Scriptures without fault, and is more pious than God—that is satanical."[12]

Luther told other stories about the devil.

When I awoke last night, the Devil came and wanted to debate with me; he rebuked and reproached me, arguing that I was a sinner. To this I replied: Tell me something new, Devil! I already know that perfectly well; I have committed many a solid and real sin. . . . [Christ] took all my sins upon Him so that now the sins I have committed are no longer mine but belong to Christ. This wonderful gift of God I am not prepared to deny, but want to acknowledge and confess.[13]

Luther believed that all the adversary's attacks were directed toward the certainty of one's salvation. Oberman writes, "All temptations, whatever sort they may be, are aimed at awakening doubts in God's reliability."[14] "The devil drives a person to doubt his own election, and seduces the doubter into wanting to penetrate God's hidden will to find out whether or not he is really among those chosen by God."[15]

Luther tells us how he dealt with the devil.

When I go to bed, the Devil is always waiting for me. When he begins to plague me, I give him this answer: "Devil, I must sleep. . . . So go away." If that doesn't work and he brings out a catalog of sins, I say, "Yes, old fellow, I know all about it. And I know some more you have overlooked." . . . If he still won't quit and presses me hard and accuses me as a sinner, I scorn him and say, "St. Satan, pray for me. Of course you have never done anything wrong in your life. You alone are holy. Go to God and get grace for yourself. If you want to get me all straightened out, I say, Physician heal thyself."[16]

Luther believed that the devil cited Moses and the Ten Commandments against the "alien righteousness" of Christ; this fiend breeds scruples, insists on good works, and relentlessly drives the conscience to assuage the wrath of a just God. Luther knew that, ultimately, the devil was God's devil who had to submit to God at all times. Imagine Luther's relief when he could say, "My sins are no longer mine but they belong to Christ!"

Yet despite this incredible despair of soul, Luther discovered that his only cure for depression was work. During these ten months he wrote about a dozen books. But more important, a copy of Erasmus's edition of the Greek New Testament was brought to him. From this edition he made a fresh translation of the New Testament into German in just eleven weeks! (The Old Testament would occupy him for the rest of his life.)

Trouble in Wittenberg

While Luther was away from Wittenberg, leadership of the Reformation fell to Philipp Melanchthon, his esteemed associate. Here the Reformation moved more quickly than Luther had wished: priests and monks got married, and the mass was no longer regarded as a sacrament but a service of thanksgiving to God.

On Christmas Day 1521, two thousand people ("the whole town," according to one chronicler) assembled in the Castle Church. Andreas Carlstadt officiated without vestments and in a plain black robe. In his sermon he told the people that in preparation for the sacrament they had no need of fasting and confession. Faith alone was all that was needed—faith, heartfelt longing, and deep contrition. "See how Christ makes you a sharer in His blessedness if you believe. See how He has cleansed and hallowed you through His promise. Still better, see that Christ stands before you. He takes from you all your struggle and doubt, that you may know that through His Word you are blessed."[17]

When Carlstadt recited the mass in Latin, he omitted all the passages about the mass as a sacrifice. The bread and the wine were given to the laity, and instructions were given in German. For the first time in their lives, the people heard in their own tongue the words, "This is the cup of my blood of the new and eternal testament, spirit and secret of the faith, shed for you to the remission of sins." One of the communicants so trembled that he dropped the bread. Carlstadt told him to pick it up, but he was so overcome by the terror of sacrilege that he couldn't bring himself to touch it again.

Then there came a new urgency: artwork and images should be removed from the churches. A riot ensued, along with the smashing of images and pictures of the saints. Carlstadt took his cue from Scripture: "Thou shalt not make unto thee any graven image, or any likeness of any thing that is in heaven above, or that is in the earth beneath, or that is in the water under the earth" (Exod. 20:4 KJV). He told the congregation about his own experience of becoming attached to images and how they diverted him from true worship. Along with this outcry against art in churches, there was an attack on music in worship. If there was to be singing during worship, it should not be more than a solo.

It was at this time that three prophets came from Zwickau (near the Bohemian border). They said that they had intimate contact with God quite apart from the Bible; in fact, they argued that if the Bible were important, God would have dropped it out of heaven. They repudiated infant baptism and proclaimed that the kingdom of God was near at hand if only proper preparation was made for its arrival. Melanchthon was moved by their zeal and wrote to Elector Frederick that they must be given an audience with Luther. "We must beware lest we resist the Spirit of God, and also lest we be possessed by the devil."[18]

Luther returned to Wittenberg in disguise, knowing that if he were recognized he could be killed. He was angered by the extremists and believed that those who demolished altars and smashed images had done the Reformation movement great harm. The Romanists had predicted that Luther would bring "division, war, and insurrection"—and now it had come to pass.

From the pulpit he preached charity and tolerance. No one can cause another to believe; no one can answer for another. Each must be fully persuaded in his or her own mind. As for the prophets from Zwickau, Luther, remembering that the Holy Spirit is represented in the New Testament as a dove, said, "I will not believe their revelations even if they have swallowed the Holy Ghost, feathers and all." He even had harsher words for them: "They boast of possessing the Spirit, more than the apostles, and yet for years now have secretly prowled about and flung around their dung. Were he a true spirit he would at once have come forward and given proof of his call by signs and words. But he is a treacherous, secret devil who sneaks around in corners until he has done his damage and spread his poison."[19] For Luther, the Word of God was the final and only authority.

Amid charges of extremism, Carlstadt left Wittenberg and spent the rest of his life in a pastorate in southern Germany. He wouldn't be the last person to be deeply disappointed in Luther for not taking his own reforms more seriously and ridding the church of all traces of Rome. Critics would say that those who followed Luther were still unable to "stamp the dust of Rome from their feet."

Be that as it may, the Reformation was in full swing. Far beyond Wittenberg changes were being made that would eventually redraw the map of Europe. People Luther denounced would start new denominations and take his reforms to extremes he had never envisioned.

When he permanently left the Wartburg Castle to return to his home in Wittenberg, Luther continued to shape the movement he had so courageously begun. There was much work to be done amid the pressure and chaos of a Germany caught up in a spiritual tug of war.

There was no turning back.

9

We Are Protestants Now

As a devout Catholic, Emperor Charles V regretted not breaking his promise of safe passage and having Martin Luther killed immediately after the Diet of Worms. From that point on, Charles would use all of his power to crush the growing Lutheran movement. But just when he thought he had the power to do so, an unexpected turn of events prevented him from fulfilling his ambitions. Charles would die with deep shame that the church he wanted to protect was now irreparably fractured.

One Faith, One King, One Law

If we ask why there was no freedom of religion during the medieval centuries, the answer lies in the fact that Europe basically accepted the dictum *Une foi, un roi, une loi*—"one faith, one king, one law." The conviction that the religion of the king was to be the religion of his subjects goes back to Old Testament times. We find it in the book of Daniel, where King Nebuchadnezzar required that all his subjects bow before his image and those who refused would be "cast into the fiery furnace."

Just so, the Roman government believed that good citizenship required that its subjects worship the emperor. This unity of religious devotion, it was believed, was necessary for the solidarity of the empire. As long as Christians believed that Jesus was one god among many and declared "Caesar is Lord," they weren't viewed as a threat to the government. But to say that "Jesus is Lord," meaning that Jesus is the *only* Lord, meant stiff penalties—for many, it meant death. The assumption was that the confession of the lordship of Caesar was necessary to maintain good citizenship and preserve political unity.

Christianity was legalized under Constantine and became the state religion a few decades later, and now that Christians were in charge of the political structures, the tables were turned. Christian emperors would come to demand that the pagans convert to Christianity. Large conversion ceremonies were held, and pagans were baptized into their new faith. Of course, for many the conversion was superficial, but they went ahead and professed Christianity at their baptism.

Infant baptism, which began in North Africa, now spread rapidly throughout Europe because it was deemed a sign of Christian unity. All who were born within the boundaries of the empire were "Christians" and hence were

Constantine, the first Christian emperor of Rome, legalized Christianity in the Roman Empire. The term "Constantinianism" refers to state support, control, or protection of Christianity.

"christened." Infant baptism was proof that the parents adhered to the religion of the empire and, of course, their children would follow suit. This explains why, when Charlemagne ruled, he demanded that any parents who refused to baptize their children be put to death. The reasons were not theological; they were political and national. Christianity was the cohesive force that unified church and state, and infant baptism was the sign of this unity. The principle of one king, one faith, and one law was firmly in place. And it was enforced.

Charles and His Challenges

With Luther's "heresy" spreading, Emperor Charles saw a threat to his vision of a unified empire. As a good Catholic, he agreed that heretics were in danger of hellfire, and so they must be killed in order to warn others who were on the same path to destruction. The problem for Charles was not only that Luther continued evading the death penalty. It was also that most Germans were siding with him, and the number of "heretics" was growing.

Charles had to consider his options. He had a number of challenges that kept him occupied and unable to deal with the German heresy. For one thing, the German princes were committed to keeping their political power within their realms—no matter the will of the emperor. Thus if they and their subjects sided with Luther, there was little Charles could do to force them to do otherwise. As mentioned earlier, the Reformation was not simply a spiritual movement; it was entwined with political issues of power and authority.

The emperor was also in conflict with the pope, who saw the aspirations of Charles as infringing on his position as head of the church. Conflict between the two escalated in 1527, when Charles captured the pope's armies and the pontiff ended up taking refuge in the Castle of St. Angelo. As the emperor's conflict with the papacy kept him occupied,

Luther's ideas kept spreading, and more princes were adopting the Lutheran faith.

Then came an even more serious challenge for Charles. Muslim Turks were camped on the outskirts of Vienna, hoping to capture the Hapsburg capital. Charles realized that he needed the cooperation of the Lutherans for an ensuing war with these ruthless invaders. He tried to balance the competing interests, but it wasn't easy.

As time progressed, Lutheranism continued to spread, and opposition to the church was empire wide. In order to bring about some kind of an appeasement of the Lutherans, two diets were held in the city of Speyer.

The Diets of Speyer

Given the political realities of the time, concessions had to be made for the growing Lutheran movement. Charles realized that the clock couldn't be turned back, at least not easily. At the first Diet of Speyer

In addition to opposing Protestantism, the Diets of Speyer also addressed taking action against the Turks, who had invaded Hungary.

in 1526, the decision was made that each ruler had to choose to be either Lutheran or Catholic "as he would have to answer to God and the Emperor." This became known as the "territorial principle"; that is, a ruler could choose either religion, and his subjects would have to follow his lead. If a Catholic found himself living in a territory with a Lutheran prince, he could move to an area ruled by a Catholic prince. The same freedom applied to the Lutherans. Hence, the medieval dictum was now reduced to "one *prince* [not king], one faith, one law." At least a measure of freedom of religion was now offered. As a result, a number of cities became Lutheran, including Strasburg, Augsburg, and Constance, which helped the followers of Luther to solidify their gains.

Charles and his Catholic supporters were not pleased with the concessions made at the Diet of Speyer. The emperor, flush with his recent victories in France and over the pope, called a second diet in Speyer three years later. Although he didn't attend this one, he hoped that he could return his empire to Catholicism by changing the previous law, even though he also sought the support of the Lutherans for his war against the Turks.

At this second Diet of Speyer in 1529, the Catholic representatives insisted that the agreement made three years earlier be nullified and a new law ratified. Territorialism was again reinforced but with a special favor given to Catholics.

Here was the change: the new law stated that Catholics in Lutheran lands had the freedom to continue in the Catholic faith despite living under a Lutheran prince, *but no Lutherans living in Catholic lands would be given similar freedom.* Lutherans in Catholic lands had to move to live under a Lutheran prince in order to practice their faith.

The Lutherans understandably resented this unfair law. They protested this injustice and hence acquired the label *Protestants.* The dissenters, in their statement, affirmed that "they must protest and testify publicly before God that they could do nothing contrary to His Word."[1] There was, at best, grudging freedom given to Lutherans.

As for other faiths, they were given no religious freedom at all. Specifically, Anabaptists and Calvinists (to be discussed in subsequent chapters) were to be put to death by drowning, fire, or sword. This dictum was enforced.

In 1529, the same year as the second Diet of Speyer, the Turks laid siege to Vienna. The gateway to the Holy Roman Empire might have fallen if the Turkish supply lines hadn't been overstretched. One of Charles's most enduring contributions to Christendom was to defeat the army of the Ottoman ruler Suleiman the Magnificent, eventually forcing the Muslim troops to return to Istanbul—but not before they would threaten Vienna again.

The Diet of Augsburg

Emperor Charles still entertained the hope that he could turn his empire back to the Catholic faith in which he so passionately believed. Hoping that each side would make some concessions, his plan was to try to unify the Catholics and Lutherans by seeking common ground between them.

In 1530, representatives from both groups were asked to meet at another Diet, this time in Augsburg, to attempt to bring unity to Germany and the empire at large. Increasingly, Charles saw himself not just as the king of Spain and the Holy Roman emperor but as one appointed by God to restore the Catholic faith to an empire that was divided by religion. He wanted to minimize doctrinal differences and see if a consensus could be reached on at least the bare essentials of the Catholic faith to reunify his empire. To his credit, he personally attended the Diet at Augsburg and put his own prestige on the line.

Luther, however, couldn't be present at Augsburg because he was still considered a fugitive from justice—the Edict of Worms was still in effect—so Philipp Melanchthon, his associate for many years in Wittenberg, represented him. Melanchthon drafted a document that attempted to stress the common elements between the two faiths in order to explore the extent to which there was agreement.

Meanwhile, Luther bided his time in the Coburg Castle, anxiously wondering what was happening at the Diet. He was evidently concerned that Melanchthon might concede too much to the Catholic representatives. But the final document, consisting of twenty-eight articles, was brought to Luther, who read it and approved its contents. "I have read Master Philip's *Apologia* [Augsburg Confession], and it pleases me very much. I know of nothing to improve or change in it."[2]

Philipp Melanchthon was a supporter of Luther throughout his life and was the first reformer to systematize Lutheran theology.

In the document, transubstantiation was denied, and though papal authority was not explicitly rejected, justification by faith was asserted. It clearly rejected the idea that we could be justified by our own strength, but rather we are "freely justified for Christ's sake, through faith. . . . This faith God imputes for righteousness in His sight."[3] On June 25, 1530, the Lutherans presented Emperor Charles with their document.

Charles listened but rejected their document. He replied by having his associates prepare a refutation of the Lutherans' position that was then presented to the Protestants with the vain hope that they would admit they were wrong. Melanchthon responded by saying that the Lutheran doctrine was based on the Scriptures, and therefore the Protestants would not recant. Predictably, the Catholics rejected Melanchthon's response.

The breach between the two groups could not be bridged by compromise, and the rift would never be healed. "Augsburg signaled that the religious divide was now unbridgeable, and the parties began to prepare for a possible war."[4] To this day, the Augsburg Confession and the later Book of Concord are the doctrinal basis of Lutheranism.

Preparing for War

Charles was down, but he wasn't out. He still had a card to play. He decided that the time would come when he could take direct action and fight against the "Lutheran protesters" and win his territories back to the Catholic faith. In fact, since he was from Spain, he knew he could recruit committed Catholic troops to crush the Protestants once and for all. But he couldn't go to war immediately; he had another distraction that needed his attention: the Turks were again threatening Vienna.

Meanwhile, Philip of Hesse, knowing that Charles would eventually move his military against the Protestants, continued his efforts to unite the "heretics." He established broad agreement within the Protestant territories and forged a formidable military force known as the Schmalkaldic League in preparation to fight the forces of Charles and his Spanish troops.

Just when a war between Catholics and Protestants seemed inevitable, the Turks returned to attack Vienna. Charles was once again forced to grant formal religious toleration to the Lutherans (this time for ten years) in exchange for military and financial support from the Protestant princes. "Thus the Schmalkaldic League [the military armies united by Phillip of Hesse] played a dangerous game—on the one hand supporting the Emperor against the Turks, while also promoting Lutheranism in Germany, Scandinavia and England."[5] As the war and time went on, more and more territories adopted the Lutheran faith.

When the threat of the Turks abated, Charles, who regretted that he was unable to squash the Protestants in the intervening years, decided that the time for military action had finally come. Several years had passed. Philip of Hesse was weakened by the fact that he had entered a bigamous marriage, and with Luther's death in 1546, the troops of the Protestant Schmalkaldic League were demoralized—it was time for Charles to attack.

Charles fought the Protestants with his imported soldiers from Spain under the command of the ruthless third Duke of Alba. One by one, German cities capitulated under the strength of Charles's army. He decisively won a victory over the Protestants in the battle of Mühlberg (east of Leipzig) in April of 1547. In fact, as a result of this victory, Charles, it is said, actually went to Wittenberg and entered the Castle Church where Luther had been buried just the year before. The Duke of Alba asked Charles to dig up the body of Luther so that it could be burned in effigy. But Charles is reported to have said, "I do not fight dead men." This account, though widely believed, has never been confirmed.

Despite the loss at Mühlberg, the Protestants rallied, and after a surprise attack, Charles's troops fled across the Alps. The victories Charles had achieved were hollow, for by then Protestantism was entrenched in many of the territories. Though Martin Luther was dead, his teachings had taken such deep root that four hundred ministers in Germany refused to comply with the Catholic victories. Catholicism could not be imposed on Germany even with the strength of a superior army.

As for Charles, he abdicated his throne in 1556 and retreated to a monastery in Spain to prepare for his death. He died lamenting that under his leadership the Catholic faith had lost its grip on an ever-increasing number of people within his empire and that he hadn't been able to crush this "heretical" movement. This emperor, who had the habit of overeating and flagellating himself for the sin, died with a candle in his right hand and a crucifix pressed to his lips with his left. His last word was "Jesus."

The Peace of Augsburg

The city of Augsburg had already played a decisive role in the Reformation. Early on, Luther had come here to debate Eck, and the doctrinal position of the Lutheran faith was defined here at a Diet. Now this city was to be the scene of another historic event.

At the Diet of Augsburg in 1555, a religious settlement gave legitimacy to the basic rule that the ruler or prince (not the emperor) determined the religion of a region. This Diet reversed the unfair law instituted at the second Diet of Speyer. Thus Lutherans were now on equal footing with Catholics. For the first time in the Christian West, two confessions, the Catholic and the Lutheran, were given equal legal recognition.[6] The religion of a given territory was still determined by its ruler, but the people were free to immigrate to whatever territory they desired.

It should be noted that this "freedom," if it can be called such, wasn't yet extended to the Reformed faith or to the Anabaptists, but it did symbolize that a state church based on a unified Christendom no longer existed.

Now that Lutheranism had achieved a position of equality alongside Catholicism, it continued to spread throughout Germany and even replaced Catholicism in the Scandinavian countries. The issues that drove this change weren't just theological; they were also political. Lutheranism gave more independence to countries that were weary of papal allegiance and paying taxes that went to Rome. In Sweden, Lutheranism became the national religion with the Augsburg Confession as its creed.

Political considerations with Norway and Denmark all contributed to a lengthy process in procuring freedom of religion for all. The seed of religious freedom planted by Martin Luther had now come into its own.

The Thirty Years' War

Europe had come a long way in granting religious freedom to Lutherans, but given the competing loyalties and ambiguity of the agreements, disputes remained. The fact that the church and the state were still intertwined meant that the issues were often complex. War erupted not just along religious lines between Catholics and Protestants but also due to various political interests and territorial disputes. These unresolved issues contributed to the Thirty Years' War.

In the midst of this conflict, the gospel was still both preached and practiced by those who had come to understand its meaning and power. For example, the Lutheran pastor Martin Rinkart served his parish in the walled city of Eilenburg in Saxony from 1617 to 1649. Many of his people became causalties of the war. Added to the war dead were many who died in the Great Pestilence of 1637. Rinkart conducted about 4,500 burial services—sometimes as many as forty or fifty a day—and yet, in 1636, he wrote the words of the familiar hymn:

> Now thank we all our God
> With heart and hands and voices;
> Who wondrous things hath done,
> In whom this world rejoices.
> Who, from our mother's arms,
> Hath led us on our way,
> With countless gifts of love,
> And still is ours today.[7]

Thankfully, the Peace of Westphalia in 1648 ended the Thirty Years' War and reaffirmed that the ruler had the right to establish the religion of the region and that people could move to whatever territory they wished. Although this peace appeared to advance the basic territorial principle that had been agreed on in previous Diets, enforcing it became impossible. This was a key turning point on the way to freedom of religion for all. Europe decided that people could choose their religion without going to war against those who held to a different faith. Even the Calvinists and the Anabaptists could now worship as they wished.

When Luther nailed his *Ninety-Five Theses* to the Castle Church door, he had no idea that his reforms would change the map of Europe and impact the Christian faith around the world. He could never have foreseen the wars, conflicts, and centuries of struggle his efforts would eventually produce. Not only was the monopoly of Catholicism finally broken, but also, as some predicted, multiple groups would be formed as the religious solidarity of the past would be splintered. The seamless garment of Christendom was torn to shreds.

Protestantism was here to stay. And for five hundred years, Catholics and Lutherans have existed side by side often with antagonism, though in recent decades there's been a growing amiable spirit. Some even have the hope that the two groups will eventually be reunited. Whether that would advance the gospel will be discussed in the last chapter of this book.

10

Disputes, Disunity, and Destiny

Martin Luther's writings had far-reaching consequences for good and for ill. Sometimes what he wrote was misinterpreted; sometimes he debated issues that would determine the theology of the Lutheran church to this day. Sometimes he wrote in anger, damaging his relationships with the Jews and other Christians for centuries to come. I've chosen to cover three of these controversies because of their ramifications throughout the five hundred years of Luther's legacy.

Controversy with the Peasants

Put yourself in the shoes of German peasants who were, in effect, slaves for their masters, the landlords. They had few rights, and although they often made their superiors rich, they didn't benefit from the prosperity they helped to create. These peasants had heard about Luther and were acquainted with his books, such as *The Freedom of the Christian*, where he argued that the Christian is a slave to no one yet serves his neighbor in love.

So these exploited peasants began an uprising. They thought that Luther, with his emphasis on Christian freedom and his relentless attacks on the church hierarchy, would surely support them. Though he identified with their plight and was well aware of the injustices done to them, he couldn't condone their revolt. Still, his name was mentioned twice in two peasant appeals used to justify their cause and right to rebellion.

Initially, Luther thought he could quell the peasants' discontent by writing *An Admonition to Peace*, in which he advised them not to justify their rebellion by misapplying the gospel. At the same time, he appealed to the princes to be more accommodating to the concerns of the peasants. He even went so far as to blame the rulers for the uprising, including the bishops and priests who "rant and rave against the holy gospel, even though you know that it is true and that you cannot refute it."[1] He rebukes them for cheating and robbing the people so that they (the rulers) could live in extravagance, then urges them to repent so they won't have to face the wrath of God.

In his treatise, Luther displays compassion to the peasants and affirms their right to hear the gospel, choose their own pastors, and the like. However, he tells them that they must take up their cause justly and with a good conscience. He warns them against violence, saying that if they killed all of their princely rulers, they would lose their soul in hell. He reminds them of Paul's strong admonition to obey the rulers that are placed over us (Rom. 13:2). He writes, "The fact that the rulers are wicked and unjust does not excuse disorder and rebellion, for the punishing of wickedness is not the responsibility of everyone, but of the worldly rulers who bear the sword."[2] Vengeance belongs to God alone, he reminded them, so they shouldn't resist with fist and sword but simply commit their grievances to the Lord. If the peasants claimed to be Christians, they must live by the law of Christ, who said, "Do not resist the one who is evil" (Matt. 5:39).

All these moderate admonitions were too late to stop the peasants' rebellion. Thus Luther, angered by the fact that his proposals were unheeded and that the peasants were justifying their violence by using the gospel, wrote the harsh treatise *Against the Robbing and Murdering Hordes of Peasants.*

In this tirade he denounces the peasants for violating their oath of obedience, creating a land filled with bloodshed and the "horrors of war" by plundering monasteries and castles that weren't theirs and blaspheming God by fighting in the name of the gospel. On these grounds, he said, they merited death, and he who was first to kill them would merit reward.

Next, in a famous, oft-quoted passage, Luther writes these bitter words.

> For rebellion is not just simple murder; it is like a great fire, which attacks and devastates a whole land. Thus rebellion brings with it a land filled with murder and bloodshed; it makes widows and orphans, and turns everything upside down, like the worst disaster. *Therefore let everyone who can, smite, slay, and stab, secretly or openly, remembering that nothing can be more poisonous, hurtful, or devilish than a rebel. It is just as when one must kill a mad dog; if you do not strike him, he will strike you, and a whole land with you.*[3]

Luther argued that, given the circumstances, the rulers were to be both judge and executioner. Rebellious peasants should be instantly judged since they had become "faithless, perjured, disobedient, rebellious murderers, robbers, and blasphemers," whom even heathen rulers had the right

Many peasants used Luther's writings to justify open rebellion. Princes used his writings to justify quashing their rebellion.

to punish.[4] If someone were to die in the process of killing them, he would die a blessed death as a martyr.

The rulers welcomed Luther's words and were all too glad to "smite, slay, and stab" the hapless peasants. Five thousand peasants were butchered, and by the time the rebellion was over, perhaps as many as one hundred thousand peasants were killed in the violence. Of course, the rulers couldn't afford to kill all the peasants because they still needed servants to till the soil and do the chores.

The peasants believed that Luther had betrayed them. He spoke of the freedom of the Christian and the need to expose and correct the injustices of the church, yet those convictions weren't applied to their plight. He was accused of justifying the cruel and vengeful acts of the rulers against these largely unarmed peasants.

During this time, Luther was under harsh criticism from both friend and foe. The peasants felt betrayed, and the Catholic rulers blamed him for the whole terrible episode, believing that his writings gave rise to the peasant unrest and subsequent revolt. From then on, Catholic rulers refused to allow Lutheran pastors into their territories, arguing that their message was one that ignited violence against the rulers.

Under pressure and harsh criticism, Luther responded with *An Open Letter on the Harsh Book against the Peasants*. The book is not an apology for what he had previously written, but rather it justifies his response. As for those who criticized him, "The rulers, therefore, ought to shake these people up until they keep their mouths shut and realize that the rulers are serious."[5] His reasoning, he said, was not based on emotional feelings of mercy for the peasants but on God's Word. The people who urged mercy for the peasants should have also insisted on mercy for the rulers. Then Luther wrote these famous words.

> There are two kingdoms, one the kingdom of God, the other the kingdom
> of the world. . . . God's kingdom is a kingdom of grace and mercy, not

of wrath and punishment. In it there is only forgiveness, consideration for one another, love, service, the doing of good, peace, joy, etc. But the kingdom of the world is a kingdom of wrath and severity. In it there is only punishment, repression, judgment, and condemnation to restrain the wicked and protect the good. For this reason it has the sword.[6]

The kingdom of this world, Luther said, should not be merciful but strict, severe, and wrathful in fulfilling its work and duty. If we confuse the two kingdoms by putting the wrath of God into God's kingdom and the mercy of God into the world's kingdom, "it is the same as putting the devil in heaven and God in hell."[7]

In other words, if we receive wrath in this world, our only duty is to submit, not to fight. Subjects have no right to attack a corrupt political ruler; they can only peacefully resist and accept whatever fate the rulers give them and accept this as the will of God. "Those who are in God's kingdom ought to have mercy on everyone and pray for everyone, and yet not hinder the kingdom of the world in the maintenance of its laws and performance of its duty; rather they should assist it."[8]

Luther rejoiced that the rebellious peasants in Germany were slaughtered because if they hadn't been, no one would be safe from their evil actions. And if the princes overreached and wantonly killed everyone without distinguishing the obedient from the rebels, God would judge them, and they would burn in hell, which was their just reward. Luther said his previous book just gave instructions for what Christian rulers should do with rebellious peasants and that it wasn't a warrant for wanton, indiscriminate slaughter. Clearly, Luther feared anarchy more than he did tyranny.

But ideas have consequences that often outlive us.

Four hundred years later, German Nazis welcomed Luther's political writings, believing that his radical separation of the two kingdoms and his emphasis on the divine origin of state authority led to an "unqualified endorsement of state power." Statements like the following appear to support this interpretation of Luther, who, when speaking about Christian soldiers, wrote, "If worldly rulers call upon them to fight, then they ought to and must fight and be obedient, not as Christians, but as members of the state and obedient subjects."[9]

By defying the authority of the church and yet giving theological justification for obedience to the God-ordained state, Luther was quoted to justify absolute obedience to the Nazi regime. His writings were interpreted to say that soldiers could kill Jews in obedience to the state, but when they were in their homes or at church they should exercise the Christian virtues of love, forgiveness, and kindness. There was one morality for the state and another for the home and church.

Luther strongly abhorred the idea of a religious war. He made it clear that he opposed the Crusades of previous centuries that took up the banner of the cross and fought to rescue the Holy Land. To take up the sword in the name of Christ was damnable. The Christian should fight on his knees, for behind the physical struggles are spiritual forces that can be overcome only by prayer.

However, if the war wasn't religious but fought by the state, it was legitimate and right for a soldier to fight. Christian soldiers thus remove themselves from the sphere of Christian morality and enter the sphere of the state with its own ethics and values.

This separation between the private morality of the home and church and the ruthless morality of the state fostered the idea that the state was free from any restraints of theology as it mapped out its policies—it had to do what it had to do. Perhaps Luther would not have agreed with this interpretation, but to the Nazis he seemed to say what they wanted to hear.

Luther's idea of "the two spheres" motivated Christian leaders such as Dietrich Bonhoeffer and Karl Barth to draft the Barmen Declaration to respond to the German churches that were complicit in the advance of Nazism. The Barmen document reads in part, "We reject the false doctrine that there are spheres of our life in which we belong not to Jesus Christ, but to other masters, realms where we do not need to be justified and sanctified by Him."[10] The church had to choose between a Christ who was Lord over a "shrinking spiritual sphere" and a Christ who was "Lord of all."

Throughout the past two thousand years, church and state have had a complex, ever-changing, and often adversarial relationship, and undoubtedly, disagreements about what that relationship should be will continue until the Lord returns. But Luther's view had implications he would not have appreciated.

Controversy regarding Predestination and Free Will

If you're a Christian, at some point you've probably participated in a discussion about predestination versus free will and may have concluded that the matter was either too complex or too irrelevant to dig further into the subject matter.[11] Since there are fine Christians on both sides of the issues, you may be tempted to conclude that the controversy is really not all that important. But for those of you who think that, Martin Luther has a word for you. He said that people who weren't interested in this issue "shall know nothing whatever of Christian matters, and shall be far behind all people upon the earth. He that does not feel this, let him confess that he is no Christian."[12] Strong words!

Why did Luther believe this issue was so essential? He was convinced that it went to the heart of the gospel. It was the "hinge" on which everything turned. *To affirm free will was to compromise grace.*

The Dispute with Erasmus

Dutch humanist Erasmus of Rotterdam thought that Luther's view should not go unchallenged, so he wrote a book critical of Luther's support of Augustine's views that the will was not free. The book,

Diatribe concerning Free Will, begins with Erasmus acknowledging that he would be criticized for attacking Luther—like a fly trying to attack an elephant. He professed great respect for Luther and believed Luther would welcome this exchange of views. Erasmus didn't think the issue was very important, but it was at least worthy of consideration. Therefore, he presented several arguments showing the rational and biblical support for free will.

Luther countered with a thunderous denunciation of Erasmus in his own book, *The Bondage of the Will.* Undoubtedly, it is Luther's best work (he himself said so) and thus deserves careful study. To read Luther is to grasp the drama, wit, and passion of lively theological dialogue. These matters that impinge on salvation and damnation touched a nerve that resulted in a brilliant defense of the gospel.

Though Luther and Erasmus never personally met, they had become friends through their writings—indeed, Erasmus had paved the way for Luther's reforms by publishing a new edition of the Greek New Testament. "Erasmus laid the egg and Luther hatched it," historians tell us.[13] But this debate ended their friendship. Luther considered Erasmus's arguments to be weak and inconsistent. "Erasmus," Luther wrote, "is an eel. Only Christ can grab him."[14]

The question wasn't if people had freedom of choice in matters pertaining to everyday life. Luther could care less whether a person had the freedom to choose to lie out in the sun or to stay indoors. Such a discussion, though interesting, had nothing to do with the gospel. At stake was the question of whether people could, *on their own,* turn away from sin to God. Also, Luther and Erasmus were talking about the willpower of the unconverted. They

Known as "Prince of the Humanists," Erasmus was a theologian, Bible translator, and admirer of Luther.

didn't address the question of whether a Christian had free will in these matters. Since believers are indwelt by the Holy Spirit, it's reasonable to suppose that they are able to exercise freedom in spiritual matters, as Augustine believed.

The debate, then, centered on whether the unconverted person could make any contribution whatsoever to his or her salvation. Does the unconverted person have the ability within his or her nature to take any step toward God, or does God, in His sovereignty, quicken those who are dead in trespasses and sins and move their wills to receive the truth of the gospel?

For Luther, even admitting that humanity can merit grace by exercising freedom of choice diminished the grace of God. If Erasmus was right, one person is converted and another is lost because there is a difference in them; the former had the good sense to exercise his or her free will and choose Christ while the latter did not. Luther would say that one person is saved and another is lost because *God alone made the difference among them.* All people are equally bound in sin. Thus if one believes the gospel, it is because God chose him or her to salvation and wrought special grace in his or her heart to bring it about.

Consider the full impact of Luther's words.

> But a man cannot be thoroughly humbled, until he comes to know that his salvation is utterly beyond his own powers, counsel, endeavors, will, and works, and absolutely depending on the will, counsel, pleasure, and work of another, that is, of God only. For if, as long as he has any persuasion that he can do even the least thing himself towards his own salvation, he retains a confidence in himself and does not utterly despair in himself, so long he is not humbled before God; but he proposes to himself some place, some time, or some work, whereby he may at length attain unto salvation. But he who . . . [depends] wholly upon the good-will of God, he totally despairs in himself, chooses nothing for himself, but waits for God to work in him; and such an one is the nearest unto grace, that he might be saved.[15]

Luther's point was that the doctrine of sovereign grace crushes human pride. When this doctrine is preached and people grasp it, they cast themselves helplessly upon God's mercy. He continues, "These things, therefore, are openly proclaimed for the sake of the Elect: that, being by these means humbled and brought down to nothing, they might be saved. The rest resist this humiliation; nay, they condemn the teaching of self-desperation; they wish to have a little something that they may do themselves. These secretly remain proud, and adversaries to the grace of God."[16]

What is really at stake here? Many evangelicals today teach that salvation is by God's grace, but God looks to us to contribute the faith by which we may be saved: we choose God; God does not choose us. So there is at least something, however small, that God looks to us for in salvation. This popular conception of the gospel was taught by Erasmus.

Luther strongly disagreed. He said that *even the faith by which a person believes is God given.* Of course, a person's will is involved in salvation, but it is God acting on the human will that causes a person to seek God. Therefore, a person is saved not because she had of herself the desire or ability to believe but because God chose her and acted on her will to bring her to faith. For Luther, salvation was wholly of the Lord.

The state of the natural person was vividly described by Luther as "bound, miserable, captive, sick, and dead, but who, by the operation of his lord Satan, to his other miseries, adds that of blindness: so that he believes he is free, happy, at liberty, powerful, whole, and alive."[17] God gives us commandments that are impossible to keep in order that we might be driven to despair and cast ourselves on His mercy. With Augustine, Luther shouted, "I ought, but I cannot!"

At this point, Luther made a distinction that was important to his theology: there is the revealed will of God and the secret, hidden purpose of God. On the one hand, God pleads with the sinner to believe;

on the other hand, He plans the damnation of many. This secret will is not to be inquired into but reverently adored.

Luther might have used the case of Abraham to make his point. God telling Abraham to slay his son was an expression of the revealed will of God, but at the same time, God was secretly planning that the boy would live. Therefore, God may give us certain commands but be planning something that, to us, seems contrary to what He commanded us to do. The clay has no right to question the potter. We have no permission to pry into the secret counsels of the Almighty but to put our hands over our mouths. As Luther said, all we can do is to stand in awe of God.

Luther was not willing to go beyond this. If someone wished to pry into God's secret will, he might choose to do so at his own peril. He wrote, "We let him go on, and, like the giants, fight against God; while we look on to see what triumph he will gain, persuaded in ourselves, that he will do nothing, either to injure our cause or to advance his own."[18]

Can Luther's view of God be reconciled with the mercy of God? Luther wrote, "This is the highest degree of faith—to believe that He is merciful, who saves so few and damns so many."[19] That God displays mercy to the elect is clear enough. As Paul said, "So then he has mercy on whomever he wills, and he hardens whomever he wills" (Rom. 9:18).

Luther continued by saying the human will is like a beast—if God sits on it, it goes where God wills; if Satan sits on it, it goes where Satan wills. The beast, however, lacks the ability to choose its own rider. The riders themselves strive to see who shall ride on the beast's back.

To clarify, when God works in the heart of the elect to bring them to faith, it's not coercion, but "the *will*, being changed and sweetly breathed on by the Spirit of God, desires and acts, not from *compulsion*, but *responsively*, from pure willingness, inclination, and accord."[20] The human will is not free but responsive to either the wickedness of the heart or the sovereign work of God, which grants to the elect the ability to accept the gospel.

The Response of the Catholic Church

How important was this dispute between Luther and Erasmus in the history of the Reformation? The Roman Catholic Church regarded the freedom of the will as *the central issue* in Luther's split with the church. In contrast to Luther, Roman Catholicism holds that humanity is not totally depraved; the fall made humanity morally sick but not dead. People can contribute to their own salvation by preparing their hearts to receive grace and by cooperating with God in the salvation process. And, as we learned in previous chapters, Catholicism taught that because people can cooperate with God in salvation, good works become indispensable in the quest for eternal life.

Perhaps the two views can be contrasted like this: Catholicism and much of evangelicalism today view humanity as drowning, and God in His grace throws us a rope. But whether a person grabs it depends on that person's own choice and disposition. And even after a person has grasped the rope, he must, by his own efforts, hang on to it.

Though Luther saw humanity as drowning, he also saw humanity as unconscious, or more accurately, spiritually dead. Hence, humanity couldn't even reach out to God's grace. God, by His own choice, has to reach down and save humanity by quickening lifeless corpses and granting them the faith to believe. Thus, salvation is wholly of God.

This dispute regarding free will versus predestination did not begin with Luther and Erasmus; there was already a long history of the argument in Christianity. And, as you might guess, their debate would not put the matter to rest. As we shall see later on, John Calvin would agree with Luther about God's sovereignty in humanity's salvation (with some minor differences). Then a man by the name of Arminius would object to the strong assertions of Luther and Calvin, and today we still speak of the Arminian-Calvinistic debate.[21]

Controversy with the Jews, or Luther's Dark Side

In his classic book *The Rise and Fall of the Third Reich*, William Shirer calls Luther a "savage anti-Semite" because he called the Jews "venomous," "bitter worms," and "disgusting vermin."[22] In 1543, near the end of his life, Luther wrote three tracts against the Jews, in which he said, "The Jews are a base, whoring people, that is, no people of God, and their boast of lineage, circumcision, and law must be accounted as filth. The Jews are full of the devil's feces . . . which they wallow in like swine, their synagogue is an incorrigible whore and an evil slut."[23]

For five centuries, his words have often been quoted by Jews as proof that Christ could not be their friend. Listen to Luther's advice as to how to treat them.

First, to set fire to their synagogues or schools and to bury and cover with dirt whatever will not burn, so that no man will ever again see a stone or a cinder of them. This is to be done in honor of our Lord and of Christendom. . . . Second, I advise that their houses also be razed and destroyed. . . . Third, I advise that all their prayer books and Talmudic writings, in which such idolatry, lies, cursing, and blasphemy are taught, be taken from them. Fourth, I advise that their rabbis be forbidden to teach henceforth on pain of loss of life and limb. Fifth, I advise that safe-conduct

When Jews were expelled from Wittenberg in 1305, an image of Jews suckling on a pig was carved on the outside upper corner of the church. In 1987, the church added a plaque to apologize for the anti-Semitism.

on the highways be abolished completely for the Jews. . . . Sixth, I advise that usury be prohibited to them, and that all cash and treasure of silver and gold be taken from them and put aside for safekeeping.[24]

Luther, how could you?

In *Mein Kampf*, Adolf Hitler commended Luther as a great reformer who was worthy to be classed with Frederick the Great and Richard Wagner. But unfortunately, Hitler didn't admire Luther for uncovering the gospel and proclaiming salvation through Christ alone by faith alone. Rather, he saw him as a man of courage who withstood the church and, more important, as one who hated the Jews.

Needless to say, Luther's comments are despicable and anti-Christian and must be strongly denounced, but we owe it to him to look at the context of his remarks. Here are some words he wrote at an earlier time when he blamed the unbelief of the Jews on the failures of medieval Christianity. We wish he had repeated these comments at the end of his life: "We must indeed with prayer and the fear of God before our eyes exercise a keen compassion towards them [the Jews] and seek to save some of them from the flames. Avenge ourselves we dare not. Vengeance a thousand times more than we can wish them is theirs already."[25]

Why the change of heart? Because Luther was incredibly naive. He actually thought that once he had uncovered the gospel, the Jews would accept Christ as Messiah en masse. When they gave no evidence of turning toward Christianity, he turned against them in anger. In Luther's last days, when the irritability of age and disease took over, he said many things that would have been best left unsaid.

Inexcusable as his remarks were, we must bear two things in mind. First, his animosity was religious, not racial. There is nothing in his writings about the purity of blood; they focus rather on the purity of doctrine. The fact that the Jews rejected Christ made him angry. As for his comments about their wealth, he believed that it had been illegally obtained through usury and thus should be confiscated and put in a fund for "believing Jews." But at root was the medieval notion that it was the responsibility of the church to hate those who hated Christ. The Jews—the "Christ killers"—thus became the target of his anger and persecution.

Second, in lashing out against the Jews, Luther was following in the footsteps of other famous Christian leaders. Justin Martyr, in his *Dialogue with Trypho*, wrote that Jewish misfortunes were divine punishment and "tribulations were justly imposed on you for you have murdered the Just One." John Chrysostrom preached eight hateful messages against the Jews.

But we must ask, what would Martin Luther have done or said if he had lived in Hitler's Germany? No doubt he would have opposed Hitler's racially motivated hatred of the Jews and condemned the Führer as antichrist. It's too bad that Hitler didn't see the other side of Luther, a man who, for all of his faults, understood the meaning of Christ's cross. Hitler understood only the meaning of his own struggle.

Whether he was right, wrong, or somewhere in between, Luther held his convictions with deep passion and expressed his views with condemning language. The man who often spoke under the inspiration of the Holy Spirit also could speak under the inspiration of the devil whom he feared. Yet, despite this, we owe a great debt of gratitude for his towering intellect, his understanding of justification by faith alone, and his singular courage.

Luther's tombstone and pulpit in the Castle Church in Wittenberg

11

Luther and the Bible

I f Martin Luther had no other accomplishment than translating the Bible into German, he would have deserved a prominent place in the stream of German history. That this enormous task was only one of his accomplishments is a tribute to his resolve and genius.

At the Diet of Worms, Luther pointedly affirmed that he did not accept the decrees of popes or traditions because they often contradicted each other. The conviction that the Bible alone was the basis for doctrine and practice now consumed him. He strongly objected to the church's decision to create a synthesis between Aristotle's philosophy and Christian theology. This reliance on "human reason" he believed, was just more proof that the church had lost its way.

The Bible reveals a God who is unknown to the philosophers. It contains that which is unexpected—a God who battles the devil by being crucified. The Holy Spirit has His own language, and one must become a student of the Scriptures in order to interpret it and discern its intended meaning. Human philosophy obscures the free offer of the gospel.

In the Wartburg Castle, with his dramatic defense at Worms still fresh in his mind, Luther turned to writing and translating. He thought his time might be short because, after all, with the Edict of Worms signed by the emperor, there were many enemies who would gladly kill him to please the emperor.

As we have already learned, Luther was given his own small room in the Wartburg, with one window, a stone floor, and a table. With his copy of Erasmus's new edition of the Greek New Testament, he went to work completing the New Testament in German—a great feat of scholarship and personal discipline. Only long hours of work enabled him to battle insomnia, confusion, and depression.

His New Testament was completed in just eleven weeks (about 1,500 words per day). For the translation of the Old Testament, he enlisted the help of others, and the project continued throughout the rest of his life. When completed, this Bible would be used to unite the German people in a common German dialect and transform the face of Christianity in Germany. Later, Luther would credit the Scriptures with bringing about the Reformation. God, he said, enabled him to do what he did through his praying and preaching. "The Word did it all."

The Method of Luther's Translation

What was so significant about Luther's translation? First, he translated the New Testament from the original Greek. Other versions, based on Latin translations, were not only difficult to read but reflected the inaccuracies of St. Jerome's Latin translation. Since the New Testament was written in Greek, Luther now had, for all practical purposes, direct exposure to the original manuscripts and thus a better understanding of the intended meaning.

In fact, the inaccuracy of previous German translations had misled the church for centuries. The Latin translation of Jesus's command in Matthew 4:17 read, "Do penance, for the kingdom of heaven is at hand." But the original Greek text reads, "Be penitent . . ." "Therefore God demanded not outward deeds

Luther's German translation of the Bible unified the German language and contributed to a growing sense of German national identity.

but a changed heart and mind. . . . 'To repent' and 'to do penance' were two different things."[1] "Doing" had nothing to do with salvation.

It's easy to see how the idea of "doing penance" gave credence to the idea that parishioners contributed to their salvation by their works, and because of that, the church prescribed "deeds of penance" as it saw fit. But to "be penitent" represents a change of heart; it's an attitude of repentance and heartfelt sorrow for sin. Luther already saw this distinction, as seen in the first point in his *Ninety-Five Theses*: "When our Lord and Master, Jesus Christ, said 'Repent ye' He intended that the whole life of believers should be penitence."

Second, Luther translated the Bible into the German vernacular, that is, into the common language of the people. He was careful to choose words that reflected a general German dialect, not nuances limited to Wittenberg. He was willing to entrust the Scriptures to the common man or woman, believing that Scripture interprets Scripture and that ordinary people would be able to understand the teachings of the Bible. He wanted the plowman and the weaver to read and recite Scriptures as they worked. He wrote, "One must ask the mother at home, the children in the street, the man at the market, and listen to how they speak, and translate accordingly. That way they will understand and notice that one is speaking German to them."[2] He objected to those who wished to "torment" the words and make them say what is not in the text.

While he worked on his translation, he made frequent visits to the butcher so that he might better understand the various parts of the animal that are referred to in the book of Leviticus. He visited jewelers to better understand the various precious stones that are mentioned in the book of Revelation. He said that he wanted Moses to speak such good German that the people wouldn't even know that he was a Jew!

Luther believed in the grammatical and historical interpretation of the Bible. He moved away from speculation and allegorical translations. However, he didn't back away from his theological convictions and freely admitted that it was his theology that helped him to do translation work. For example, in Romans 3:28 we read, "For we hold that one is justified by faith apart from works of the law." Luther added the little word "alone." Thus it read, "We are justified by faith *alone*." He was criticized for adding a word to the text, but he defended it by saying that such an addition was necessary to bring out the clarity of the apostle Paul's thought.

Disputes about the Extent of the Canon

The Reformers reopened the debate regarding the extent of the canon, since many of the books that Protestants call the Apocrypha were included within the pages of the Bibles that were currently in use. These books found their way into the Bible because St. Jerome had reluctantly inserted them into his Latin translation. This translation became the Bible of Christendom for a thousand years. Actually, not even the Catholic Church believed that these books had the same authority as the other books of the Old Testament. The complete validity of these apocryphal books was not even affirmed by the Catholic Church until the Council of Trent met to bring about some basic reforms in 1546 (four years after Luther's death). Many Protestants suspect that the reason these books were given this new exalted status is because some of their content could be used against the doctrine of justification by faith alone.

Reformers believed that the true ground of canonicity was rooted in the intrinsic quality and teachings of the books, which, according to Luther, meant that the doctrine of justification was a central criterion for canonicity. The church, Luther believed, should be placed under the authority of the Bible rather than standing above it and adding its various papal pronouncements as it saw fit.

Luther therefore made a distinction between the more important and less important books of the Bible "according to their evangelical piety and force."[3] He put Hebrews, James, Jude, and Revelation at the end of the German Bible, and in his introduction gave this explanation: "Hitherto we have had the right and genuine books of the New Testament. The four that follow have been differently esteemed in olden times."[4]

Luther disliked the book of James because he could not harmonize it with Paul's teaching on justification by faith without works. So he called it "an epistle of straw" in contrast with other genuine writings. (Luther borrowed this terminology from Jeremiah the prophet, who spoke of those who gave their own visions as straw compared to wheat; see Jer. 23:28.) However, Luther's remarks should not be overstated. He was not blind to the fact that James was a teacher of practical Christianity, but he was responding to the fact that James said nothing about the cross or resurrection.

He objected to Hebrews because it seemed to deny the possibility of repentance after baptism; he thought the Epistle of Jude was unnecessary since it seemed to be a duplicate of 2 Peter; and he could find no sense in the mysteries of the book of Revelation because the apocalypse dealt only with images and visions.

In retrospect, Luther clearly misunderstood these four books whose interpretation and purpose seemed obscure to him. James can be reconciled with Paul; Hebrews can be reconciled with all the various modes of baptism; and although Jude has essentially the same content as 2 Peter, it does have unique characteristics. As for Revelation, though it has many visions and analogies, it highly exalts Christ and vividly reminds us of His glorious return.

The matter of the canon still divides Catholics and Protestants. When Johann Eck debated Luther, he made this point: "The Scriptures are not authentic, except by the authority of the church." In other words, the church can confer authenticity on a book, or it can, and often does, elevate tradition above Scriptures. Truth is whatever the official teaching of the church says it is.

The Second Vatican Council (Vatican II), a conference held in 1962–65, summarized the official position of the church on this issue: "It is clear therefore, that sacred tradition, Sacred Scripture and the teaching authority of the Church . . . are so linked and joined together that one cannot stand without the others, and that all together and each in its own way under the action of the Holy Spirit contribute effectively to the salvation of souls."[5]

Protestants stress that a book either does or does not have inherent authority; it is either from God or it is not. For example, a letter written by Abraham Lincoln would be authentic even if historians did not recognize it as such. And if he didn't write the letter, all the councils and pronouncements of men could not make it become a letter from his hand.

In other words, if a book of the Bible was inspired by God, it would be authoritative even if Old Testament Israel and the New Testament church failed to recognize it as such. And if it wasn't inspired by God, it wouldn't matter how sincerely God's people believed it was of divine authorship because it still wouldn't have authority. My point is that we must distinguish between the *authority* of a particular book and the *recognition* of that authority.

Protestants boldly affirm that it was a fallible church that chose what we believe to be an infallible list of books that composes our Bible. Yes, theoretically, the church might have erred for one reason: *the church is fallible; the Scriptures are not.*

Having said that, we do not believe that the church erred. First, there are no additional books in existence that make a serious claim for the New Testament canon. Even those canonical books whose acceptance was disputed have proved their worth, and the books that were excluded have been shown to be subbiblical. To the person who says that the church erred, we reply, "Set forth your case; give us your recommendations as to which book should be removed and which books, if any, should be included." At that point, the discussion usually ends.

Second, as already argued above, we believe that God providentially preserved His Word. He did this, however, not by making the church infallible in all of its official decisions but by guiding His own people to recognize those books that had the stamp of divine authority.

Are you still troubled by the thought that it was a fallible church that selected what we believe to be infallible Scriptures? You should not be surprised. After all, it was fallible human beings who wrote the infallible Scriptures. King David in the Old Testament and Peter in the New serve as examples.

Luther's Reverence for the Scriptures

Regardless of his misgivings about four of the books of the New Testament, Luther highly revered the Scriptures and believed that we must seek to understand them and submit to their authority. Perhaps we can best appreciate Luther's high view of the Bible if we simply quote what he had to say about the text of Scripture.

This I can say with good conscience: I have used the utmost faithfulness and care in this work, and I never had any intention to falsify anything. I have not taken nor sought nor want a single penny for it. Neither do

I intend to win honor by it (that God, my Lord knows); but I did it as a service to the dear Christians and to the honor of the One who sits above, who does so much good to me every hour that if I had translated a thousand times as much or as diligently, I still should not deserve to live a single hour or to have a sound eye. All that I am and have is due to His grace and mercy, aye, to His precious blood and bitter sweat. Therefore, God willing, all of it is to be done to His honor, joyfully and sincerely. If scribblers and papal jackasses abuse me, very well, let them do so. But pious Christians and their Lord Christ praise me; and I am too richly repaid if only a single Christian recognizes me as a faithful worker.[6]

He who carefully reads and studies the Scriptures will consider nothing so trifling that it does not at least contribute to the improvement of his life and morals, since the Holy Spirit wanted to have it committed to writing. We see with what great diligence Moses, or rather the Holy Spirit, describes even the most insignificant acts and sufferings of the patriarchs.[7]

We ought not to criticize, explain, or judge the Scriptures by our mere reason, but diligently with prayer, meditate thereon and seek their meaning. The devil and temptations also afford us occasion to learn and understand the Scriptures by experience and practice. Without these we should never understand them, however diligently we read, and listened to them. The Holy Ghost must here be our only master and tutor; and let youth have no shame to learn of that preceptor.[8]

A fiery shield is God's Word; of more substance and purer than gold, which, tried in the fire, loses naught of its substance, but resists and overcomes all the fury of the fiery heat; even so, he that believes God's Word overcomes all, and remains secure everlastingly, against all misfortunes; for this shield fears nothing, neither hell nor the devil.[9]

Later he said, "I simply taught, preached, and wrote God's Word. . . . And while I slept or drank Wittenberg beer with my friends Philip and

Amsdorf, the Word so greatly weakened the papacy that no prince or emperor ever inflicted such losses on it. I did nothing; the Word did everything."[10]

Luther's Method of Study

Luther spent his life trying to clarify the Scriptures, especially those that were crucial to the doctrine of salvation. He said that studying the Bible should be like going on a journey full of surprising discoveries. Comparing his scriptural studies to a sojourn through the forest, he said, "There is hardly a tree in this forest that I have not shaken and obtained apples or picked berries from."[11] The devil's battle against Christ makes this walk through the woods essential. Luther believed that laypeople had to be knowledgeable of the Bible because, after all, they had to see for themselves what they believed.

The Bible is not one book but a library of books whose reach has extended through two millennia. Regarding the central truth of the Bible, Luther said to Erasmus, "Through the Crucified One, the Christian knows everything he has to know, but he now knows what he cannot know."[12]

"Whoever wants to read the Bible must make sure he is not wrong, for the Scriptures can easily be stretched and guided, but no one should guide them according to his emotions, he should lead them to the well, that is to the cross of Christ, then he will certainly be right and cannot fail."[13]

The Historical and National Effects of Luther's Translation

As I mentioned previously, if the translation of the Bible into German was Luther's only accomplishment, he would have already gone down in history as a great benefactor to the German nation. We must remember that during that time, Germany was a conglomeration of territories with varying weights and measures and without a common dialect. Luther translated the Bible into the language he heard on the street in his own town of Wittenberg and also asked others to help him choose the words that would be best known to a majority of the Germans.

Luther understood that biblical truth could be powerfully communicated through song. "A Mighty Fortress Is Our God" is his best-known hymn.

In her book *German: Biography of a Language*, Ruth H. Sanders says that Luther was so successful with translating the book not only into German but also into the vernacular of the time that a Catholic opponent complained that "even tailors and shoemakers . . . read it with great eagerness."[14] A reviewer of Sanders's book in the August 5, 2010, edition of *The Economist* writes, "Rarely has a single man had such a mark on a language. The German of Luther's Bible was nobody's native language in his day. Today it is so universal that it threatens Germany's once vibrant dialects with death by standardization."[15]

Consider this assessment:

> Luther magnified the inherent potency of his ideas by articulating them in a language that was without rival in clarity and force. He strove to make the Scriptures accessible to ordinary worshipers by translating them into vernacular German. This he did with such genius that the German dialect he used became the written language of all of Germany. Without Luther's translation of the Bible, Germany might have come to use a number of mutually incomprehensible languages, as was the case in the northwestern part of the Holy Roman Empire, where local dialects evolved into what is now modern Dutch. Luther also wrote hymns that are still sung in Christian religious services all over the world.[16]

Gutenberg had introduced the printing press in Mainz in the 1400s, and now copies of the Bible were quickly spreading throughout Germany. The Bible would not just be accessible to churches but to anyone who could read. Martin Luther's vision of the plowman and the weaver having access to the Scriptures was coming to pass.

12

Luther, Katie, Children, and Death

When Martin Luther took his vows of celibacy in the monastery in Erfurt, he was certain that he would never marry. But when he was excommunicated by the church, his mentor and confessor Johann Staupitz released him from those vows. The monk turned reformer was now free to marry but still did not intend to do so. Luther, who expected to be put to death at any moment, thought marriage would be unfair to his wife, who would almost surely be widowed.

But events took an interesting turn when Luther was staying in the Wartburg Castle. Monks in Wittenberg, having renounced their own vows of celibacy, were marrying nuns who were leaving their cloisters. Tracts about the gospel, written by Luther, had made it into the nunnery near Torgau, and Luther was giving the nuns advice on how they might escape. This was not only a violation of the law but was also regarded as a capital offense; however, Luther believed that his prince, Elector Frederick the Wise, would probably look the other way—and he did.

Luther made an arrangement with Leonard Kopp, who from time to time delivered barrels of herring to the convent in Torgau. In 1523, Kopp bundled twelve nuns, hid them behind barrels (some accounts say they were hiding *in* the empty barrels), and took them to Wittenberg in his covered wagon. Three of the nuns returned to their homes, but nine stayed in Wittenberg. A student reported to a friend, "A wagon load of vestal virgins has just come to town, all more eager for marriage than for life. God grant them husbands lest worse befall."[1] These women knew very little about living in the real world. One person commented, "All that they can do is sing and pray."

Luther felt it was his responsibility to find them husbands or homes. Someone suggested that he marry one himself; he commented that he had no such intention because he expected daily to die the death of a heretic. In the end, all were provided for except for Katherine von Bora. Luther made several suggestions for men whom she might marry, but she was uninterested. She had her eye on a man who had come to lecture at Wittenberg—Dr. Nickolas Amsdorf. In talking with Amsdorf, she asked him to tell Luther that she could not accept the men Luther had suggested, but if she did marry, it would have to be either Amsdorf himself or Luther. (She said this in jest because she believed these men were ineligible; also, by this time both men were in their forties.)

Luther visited his parents, and they encouraged him to marry Katie. His father, who opposed his son's decision to enter the monastery, thought marriage would be a good idea. Luther had been teaching that the institution of marriage was divinely established and should be elevated above celibacy, and slowly the idea began to grow on him. Even if he were to die at the stake, his marriage would give status to Katie, and he could affirm his faith.

One of Katherine's key contributions to the Reformation was to help model Protestant marriage and illustrate the value of marriage for clergy.

Finally, he gave three reasons for his marriage: to please his father, to spite the pope and the devil, and to seal his witness before martyrdom. He was betrothed to Katie on June 13, 1525. In those days, a betrothal was the equivalent of marriage, yet on June 27, a public ceremony was held. (The ceremony is reenacted annually in the Wittenberg Town Square, a joyful tradition celebrated in June.)

Luther sent out invitations. To George Spalatin he wrote, "You must come to my wedding. I have made the angels laugh and the devils weep." Spalatin asked him what he thought of long courtships, and Luther replied, in effect, "Don't put off until tomorrow what you can do today!" He invited Kopp, who had arranged the escape of the nuns, but he did not get a response. Apparently he sent a second invitation to Kopp, "My lord Katie and I invite you to send a barrel of the best Torgau beer, and if it is not good you will have to drink it all yourself."[2]

At ten o'clock in the morning, Luther led Katie through Wittenberg to the sound of bells to the parish church, and the ceremony took place at the portal. Some predicted that this would be the end of Luther's influence as a reformer. But, in many respects, it was just the opposite. Luther's marriage and family provided a model of how couples in ministry can serve in partnership with mutual respect and blessing. Luther did not die the death of a martyr as he thought he might, and he and Katie spent twenty-one years together.

Life with Katie

Luther and Katie were well suited for each other. Their home was filled with humor and mutual respect. "Next to God's Word, there is no more precious treasure than holy matrimony. God's highest gift on earth is a pious, cheerful, God-fearing, home-keeping wife, with whom you may live peacefully, to whom you may entrust . . . your goods and body and life."[3]

Marriage brought many changes. He admitted that before he got married, his bed hadn't been made for an entire year and was foul with sweat, but because he worked so hard and was so weary, he didn't notice it. Luther also said that when he married, he wasn't infatuated with Katie, but throughout the years, their love for each other grew. "I would not exchange Katie for France or for Venice, because God has given her to me and other women have worse faults."[4]

He had married a woman who was obviously strong willed, capable, and able to spar with her famous husband. One day when he was depressed, she dressed in dark clothing as if going to a funeral. When Luther asked her who had died, she said, "Why God has died, did you not hear the news?" Luther then began to laugh realizing how foolish he was to be discouraged, acting as if God were dead.

He often referred to Katie as "my rib" and also "my lord" (she was of noble birth). Sometimes he made a pun of her name calling her my

"*Kette*" (German for "chain"), and called himself her "willing servant." They began their lives together with no money, though they were later supported by the elector.

Katie was enterprising, looking after pigs and chickens, planting a garden, managing an orchard, and the like. In addition, she had to look after Luther, who suffered from all manner of illnesses: gout, insomnia, hemorrhoids, constipation, dizziness, and ringing in the ears.

She served him beer (which she brewed herself) as a sedative for insomnia. He paid her the highest tribute when he called St. Paul's Epistle to the Galatians "my Katherine von Bora." Again he said, "In domestic affairs I defer to Katie. Otherwise I am led by the Holy Ghost." He was, apparently, worried over too much devotion. "I give more credit to Katherine than to Christ, who has done so much more for me." Marriage, Luther said, was far better than celibacy as a school for character.

Katie ran the household and took care of the finances. Her husband never learned how to handle money. He said, "God divided the hand into fingers so that money would slip through." He would give away everything that was not absolutely necessary for them to keep. At times Katie had to hide the money to keep him away from it.

The couple inherited a farm two days' journey from Wittenberg, so Katie was often gone, attending to business there. Luther, perhaps with some resentment, wrote to her when she was away tending to the farm, "To the rich lady of Zulsdorf, who lives in the flesh at Wittenberg, but in the spirit at Zulsdorf." Some marriages, said Luther, were motivated by mere lust, but his had grown into love. He said, "The wife should make her husband glad to come home and let him make her sorry he leaves."

Dinner with the Luthers

Katie, of course, had maidservants to help her with many of her responsibilities. The Luther home was almost always open for students and friends who would stop by. After a hearty meal and some beer, the conversation would turn to theology, the pope, or the other current events of the day. Some students wrote down Luther's thoughts and answers to questions. These have come down to us today as the *Table Talks*, with 6,596 entries collated by students after his death. These writings contain many witty remarks such as,

> The monks are the fleas on God Almighty's fur coat.

> I am a pillar of the pope. After I am gone he will fare worse.

> Germany is the pope's pig. That is why we have to give him so much bacon and sausages.

> Birds lack faith. They fly away when I enter the orchard, though I mean them no ill will. Even so do we lack faith in God.[5]

Luther chided Katie for her worry about his health and safety. "You worry yourself about your God, just as if He were not Almighty, and able to create ten Doctor Martin Luthers for the old one drowned perhaps in the Saale [a river in east-central Germany], or fallen dead by the fire-place. . . . I have a better protector than you and all of the angels. He—my

Title page and portrait from a 1581 edition of Martin Luther's *Table Talks*

Protector—lies in the manger and hangs upon a Virgin's breast, but He sits also at the right hand of God, the Father Almighty. Rest, therefore, in peace. Amen."[6]

In his will dated 1542, seventeen years after he and Katie were married, he calls her a "pious, faithful, and devoted wife, full of loving, tender care."[7]

The Children: Joys and Sorrows

When their first son, Hans, was cutting teeth, Luther said that he was making a joyous nuisance of himself. "These are the joys of marriage of which the pope is not worthy." Hans often gave them trouble, struggling with obedience. Luther wrote to a prospective godmother regarding their second child, a daughter, "Dear lady, God has produced from me and my wife, Katie, a little heathen. We hope you will be willing to come and become her spiritual mother."

While staying in the Coburg Castle, unable to attend the Diet of Augsburg in 1530, Luther struggled with anxiety. He wondered whether Melanchthon would concede too much in order to please Emperor Charles V, who was attempting to unite the Lutherans with Catholicism. Despite his anxiety, Luther took the time to write this touching letter to his four-year-old son, Hans. Here are a few excerpts.

> I am glad to know that you learn well and pray hard. Keep on, my lad, and when I come home, I'll bring you a whole fair. I know a lovely garden where many children in golden frocks gather rosy apples under the trees, as well as pears, cherries, and plums. They sing, skip, and are gay. And they have fine ponies with golden bridles and silver saddles. I asked the gardener who were these children, and he said, "They are the children

Luther making music with his family

who like to pray and learn and be good." And I said, "Good man, I too have a son, and his name is Hans Luther. Couldn't he come into the garden too?" . . . And the man said, "If he likes to pray and learn and be good, he too may come into the garden."

So, my darling son, study and pray hard and tell Lippus and Jost [the sons of Melanchthon] to do this too, that you all may come together into the garden. May the dear God take care of you. Give my best to Auntie Lena and give her a kiss for me.[8]

Through his children Luther learned about God. It helped him to understand the words, "Our Father who art in heaven." A child could nurse contentedly on his mother's breast despite the chaos in the world, an example of the faith of God's children. The Luthers had six children in all: Hans, Elizabeth, Magdalena, Martin, Paul, and Margaretha. Two of their daughters died young. They also reared four orphaned children whose parents had died in the plague; along with these, other children came to live with them in the cloister. Their fourth son, Paul, became a doctor to Elector Jonas, who succeeded Elector Frederick.

When Christmas came around, Luther took a cue from his children and celebrated with childlike joy. A familiar scene was the family singing Christmas carols, including his own hymn, which included the phrase, "Good news from heaven the angels bring / Glad tidings to the earth they ring."[9]

Personal Sorrow

At only fourteen years old, Magdalena, Luther's affectionate and favorite daughter, was on her deathbed. Luther prayed, "O God, I love her so, but thy will be done." And turning to her, "*Magdalenchen*, my little girl, you would like to stay with your father here and you would be glad to go to your Father in heaven?" And she said, "Yes, dear father, as God wills." He held her in his arms until she died; then he said, "*Du liebes Lenchen* [an endearing nickname], you will rise and shine like the stars and the sun. How strange it is to know that she is at peace and all is well, and yet to be so sorrowful."[10]

Luther was fifty-nine when Magdalena died, and her death came at a time when he was going through other trials. His sorrow over losing her was often mixed with joy knowing that she was with God. To his friend Jonas he wrote, "You will have heard that my dearest child is born again into the eternal kingdom of God. We ought to be glad at her departure, for she is taken away from the world, the flesh, and the devil; but so strong is natural love, that we cannot bear it without anguish of heart, without the sense of death in ourselves."[11]

On her tombstone he inscribed these words:

> Here do I Lena, Luther's daughter, rest,
> Sleep in my little bed with all the blessed.
> In sin and trespass I was born;
> Forever would I be forlorn,
> But yet I live, and all is good—
> Thou, Christ, didst save me with thy blood.[12]

It's difficult for us today to understand the great impact Luther's marriage had on future generations. One historian put it this way: "Luther and Katie changed the way the Western world thought about marriage. Luther's advocacy for married clergy and his own example inaugurated a social reformation every bit as momentous—perhaps more so—than the ecclesiastical reformation."[13]

Keep in mind that for more than a thousand years, celibacy was upheld as an ideal, and Augustine had argued that sex, even in marriage, involved sin. Martin and Katie taught future generations that marriage involves mutual love, joyful sex, and genuine companionship—and the approval of God.

Lessons in Life and Death

When the plague made its way to Wittenberg, many people fled, fearing for their lives. Luther wrote an essay on whether a Christian should stay to help the sick or flee to safety. His answer, in brief, was that it's a matter of conscience. We should not judge those who leave if they have no responsibilities that would obligate them to stay. But if one was a town magistrate or had responsibilities, he should stay and help the sick, and if he were to die in doing so, he'd die doing God's will. Thanks to Christ, Luther believed, we can taunt death, for it has no power over us. Regarding himself during this time, he said that because he was rotund he would "give the worms plenty to feed on." Although others fled, the Luthers stayed on and helped the sick in Wittenberg.

When Luther was ill and thought he would die, he admonished Katie, "If it be God's will accept it." To which she replied, "My dear Doctor, if it is God's will I would rather have you with our Lord than here. Don't worry about us, God will take care of us."

And finally, returning home with his sons from a trip to settle a dispute, Luther died in the town of Eisleben, about a half-mile from the church where he was baptized. Years earlier in Worms he had said, "If I had a thousand heads, I would rather have them all cut off one by one than make one recantation." Now on his deathbed, he was asked if he was dying in the faith he had professed. He answered yes, and could say, "I was fearless, I was afraid of nothing; God can make one so desperately bold."[14]

Luther's Last Sermon

In 2010, I led a tour group to the sites of the Reformation. We were able to visit the church in Eisleben, and I was allowed to preach from the pulpit where Luther preached his last sermon. As providence would have it, I had a copy of his last sermon with me. I had the honor of being able to preach a few paragraphs of it from the same pulpit where he preached it! He preached this sermon on February 15, 1546, using the text from Matthew 11:25–26: "At that time Jesus declared, 'I thank you, Father, Lord of heaven and earth, that you have hidden these things from the wise and understanding and revealed them to little children; yes, Father, for such was your gracious will.'"

I quote a few paragraphs, reminding us of the relevance of his words for today. I have made a few edits in these paragraphs for the sake of clarity.

> This is a fine Gospel and it has a lot in it. Let us talk about part of it now, covering as much as we can and as God gives us grace.
>
> The Lord here praises and extols his heavenly Father for having hidden these things from the wise and understanding. That is, He did not make His gospel known to the wise and understanding, but to infants and children who cannot speak and preach and be wise. Thus He indicates that He is opposed to the wise and understanding and dearly loves those who are like young children.
>
> But to the world it is very foolish and offensive that God should be opposed to the wise and condemn them, when, after all, we have the idea that God could not reign if He did not have wise and understanding people to help Him. . . . Everything that God does they must improve, so that there is no poorer, more insignificant and despised disciple on earth than God; He must be everybody's pupil, everybody wants to be His teacher.
>
> But this behavior is a disgusting thing, and should not God grow impatient with it? Should He be so greatly pleased with these fellows who are all too smart and wise for Him and are always wanting to send Him back to school? Things are in a fine state, indeed, when the egg wants to be wiser than the hen. A fine governance it must be when the children want to rule their father and mother, and the fools and simpletons see themselves as the wise people. You see, this is the

reason why the wise and understanding are condemned everywhere in the Scriptures.

The devil has slobbered us with fools. . . . So the pope, too, wants to be a very wise man, indeed, the wisest of the wise, simply because he has a high position and claims to be the head of the church; whereupon the devil so puffs him up that he [the pope] imagines that whatever he says and does is pure divine wisdom and everybody must accept and obey it, and nobody should ask whether it is God's Word or not.

But this, God will not tolerate. He has no intention of being a pupil; they are to be the pupils. . . .

Lo, this means that the wise of this world are rejected, that we may learn not to think ourselves wise, but to cling only to Christ's Word and come to Him, as He so lovingly invites us to do, and say: Thou alone art my beloved Lord and Master, I am thy disciple.

This and much more might be said concerning this Gospel, but I am too weak and we shall let it go at that.[15]

Luther preached for what must have been a total of about thirty to thirty-five minutes, and in conclusion admitted that he was "too weak" to say more. He left the church, walked across the street to his room, became sick, and died a few days later.

Luther's body was taken back to Wittenberg with crowds lining the streets in the towns along the way. He was buried in the Castle Church where he had nailed his *Ninety-Five Theses* so many years before. On his tombstone are the simple words (in abbreviated Latin): "Here is buried the body of the Doctor of Sacred Theology,

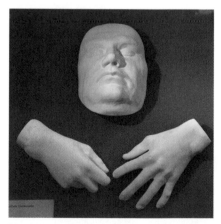

Martin Luther died on February 18, 1546, at the age of 62.

Martin Luther, who died in the year of Christ 1546, on February 18th, in his hometown Eisleben."

Four years later, Katie died, and her last recorded words were, "I will stick to Christ as a burr to a topcoat." She is buried in Torgau, the town where she had once been in a nunnery. As a single woman confined to the rigorous rules of medieval discipline, she could never have dreamed that someday she would marry one of the most famous men in history and be remembered by millions as an outstanding, hardworking, God-fearing wife and mother.

Years earlier when Luther was reflecting on his own unexpected and remarkable life, he once remarked, "Who could have seen all these things in the stars?"

Martin and Katie taught us not only how to live and love but also how to die. In the end, both humbly bowed to accept God's will in all things, including the inevitability of death. Even today their example of love and hard-won partnership is an inspiration to us all.

13

Zwingli

Reforming Zurich

I f you visit the Grossmünster (Great Cathedral) in Zurich, Switzerland, you'll see the following inscription: "The Reformation of Huldrych Zwingli began here on January 1, 1519." In a nearby church, you'll also see a statue of the reformer with a Bible in one hand and a sword in the other, symbolizing Zwingli's dual commitment to God and to the state. He would, as we'll find out, take up a sword and die as a chaplain as he encouraged the Swiss troops who were fighting a war against the Catholics.

Zwingli was born in the Swiss Alps seven weeks after Martin Luther. When he began to seriously apply himself to the study of the New Testament, he resolved to preach nothing but the gospel. This was his stance when he accepted a call to become the priest of the Grossmünster in Zurich. Although still technically a part of the Holy Roman Empire, the Swiss Confederation had gained a measure of independence by the sixteenth century.

His duties began on January 1, 1519, and this new pastor shocked his congregation by announcing his intent to abandon the traditional methods of worship. His sermons would not follow the prescribed lectionary. Instead, he would begin preaching with the Gospel of Matthew and continue on through the New Testament. This created an enthusiastic stir among his congregation, since no one had ever taught the Word of God to them systematically before.

Just two years before this, Martin Luther nailed his *Ninety-Five Theses* to the door of the Castle Church in Wittenberg. Obviously, Zwingli was aware of Luther's work in Wittenberg and admired his courage, referring to him as "an Elijah." He urged his congregation to buy and read Luther's books, but he refused to accept the label of "Lutheran" and denied dependence on Luther. Zwingli said, "I did not learn my doctrine from Luther, but from God's Word itself." He looked to the Scriptures, not to Luther, for his understanding of the gospel.

In Zwingli's first year of ministry, a terrible plague swept through Zurich, and more than two thousand of its seven thousand inhabitants died. Zwingli himself nearly died. As a result, he wrote what is known as "The Plague Song."

> Help me, O Lord,
> My strength and rock;
> Lo, at the door

Statue of Zwingli in front of the Wasserkirche (Water Church) in Zurich

I hear death's knock.
Uplift thine arm,
Once pierced for me,
That conquered death,
And set me free.

When he recovered from his near-death experience, he wrote,

My God! My Lord!
Healed by Thy hand,
Upon the earth
Once more I stand.
Let sin no more
Rule over me;
My mouth shall sing
Alone of Thee.[1]

And so this man who survived the plague inaugurated a reformation that would impact his city, his country, and even the world. Like Martin Luther, Zwingli rejected papal authority and preached justification by faith alone, denying the merit of the saints and indulgences. He also believed in predestination and that the seven sacraments should be reduced to just two.

By the early 1520s, Zwingli could no longer retain his status as a priest in the Roman Catholic Church. In 1520, he renounced the papal pension he'd been receiving, and two days later, he resigned his office as "People's Priest of Zurich." Yet surprisingly, the city council promptly hired him as the lead preacher to the entire city. Now he was in a position to press for official reforms. He challenged his critics, who accused him of abandoning the holy mother church to "leave the asses and come over to the oxen, abandon goats for the sheep." For Zwingli and his followers, the die was cast.

In 1522, Zwingli was attending a supper during Lent when two dried sausages were cut up, and the men each ate a small piece. That sounds very innocuous to us, but back then, when word of this got out, there was a backlash; meat was not to be eaten during Lent. The offenders were examined by a town council, and the matter sparked fighting in the streets. Although Zwingli himself did not eat the meat, he defended those who did and preached a message on why Christians are able to eat all foods. Given the matters swirling around him, Zwingli was forced to defend his views against mounting Catholic opposition.

The Great Disputations

Zwingli needed to address his opponents. Three "great disputations" were held where his detractors could examine his reforms. On Thursday morning, January 29, 1523, some six hundred people crowded into the Zurich town hall for the first Zurich Disputation. Zwingli simply laid Bibles in Latin, Greek, and Hebrew on the table before him. The meeting was called to order, and anyone who wished to accuse Zwingli was invited to speak. No other judge was needed, said Zwingli, except the Word of God.

Zwingli publicized sixty-seven points of contention with the Roman Catholic Church. The council not only accepted Zwingli's document but also encouraged the pastor to continue his preaching. Zwingli was publicly vindicated of the heresy charge and his Sixty-Seven Articles constituted the first Reformed confession of faith. When accused of preaching a new doctrine, he replied, "What is the gospel? Why, that is 1,522 years old." His point was that the gospel was as old as the New Testament. Some people were angry, but no one refuted him.

But much more work was to be done, and in October of 1523, a second disputation was held—this one dealing with the question of images and the mass. Zwingli now attacked the mass as "a blasphemous undertaking, a very work of anti-Christ. Christ our Redeemer gave us this only as a food and a memorial of His offering and His covenant." What is more, Zwingli rejected the real presence of Christ in the sacrament. "There would be no physical partaking of God who must be worshiped only in spirit."[2]

Despite the enthusiastic response to his preaching, the actual reforms themselves were not immediately implemented. The images and idols remained in churches until June of 1524, and the mass wasn't abolished until 1525. By the time the third disputation was over, the churches were cleared of images, the people had permission to eat meat during Lent, and priests were allowed to marry. Indeed, Zwingli himself petitioned the local bishop for permission to marry—he judged that the majority of the priests, nuns, and monks were not chaste anyway—and confessed that he too was an offender. Thus the break with the traditions of the church and papacy was complete.

Although Zwingli played six musical instruments, he not only removed the images and artifacts but also forbade the use of the organ (some reports say that it was smashed) because there was no reference to the instrument in the New Testament. Obviously, the church services lost their liturgical character. The people were to give ear to the Word of God alone. People who did not attend church were encouraged to do so; loitering was forbidden, and attendance was recorded. Catholics were permitted to stay in Zurich, but they were not allowed to participate in its government.

Zwingli also believed in election, that God, from all eternity, predestined some people to

The home in the Canton of St. Gallen where Zwingli was born

belong to the company of the redeemed. The elect could be known only through their faith in Christ. But unfortunately this doctrine, combined with his intense nationalism, led him to think of "the whole town of Zurich, save for a few Catholics, as the elect company of the Lord."[3] This meant that personal faith was often de-emphasized, since God's election appeared to extend to all the citizens of Zurich. The church was therefore best described as the New Israel of God, seen most clearly in—yes, you guessed it—Zurich.

Obviously, the question of what constituted the true church was unclear. On the one hand, people were saved through personal faith in Christ; on the other hand, whole towns in Switzerland were considered "the elect." Church historian Roland Bainton said that the test of predestination was faith, "but faith was so far diluted that it could be made coterminous with a Swiss town. There was danger that the elect would become the elite."[4]

Since Zwingli's relationship with his bishop was severed, he began to rely more directly on the town council, even agreeing that they had the right to reappoint him when his term had expired. This close association with the town council would lead Zwingli down a dangerous path. In the next chapter we'll learn that he would eventually stand beside the Limmat River and agree to the drowning of his close friends simply because they were baptized by immersion.

Given Zwingli's reputation as a teacher, he and Luther would have obvious differences. The question was whether those differences could be resolved.

Controversy about the Lord's Supper

When Martin Luther broke with Rome, he stressed that the value of the Lord's Supper was dependent on the faith of the recipient.[5] He also modified his belief in transubstantiation and taught what is often called the "real presence," or *con*substantiation. Christ was literally present in the elements, but the wine remained wine, and the bread remained bread. Thus he held to the mystery of literalness without the transformation.

With the possibility that the Catholics might be strategizing for war in order to retrieve Lutheran lands, Philip of Hesse attempted to unite the Reformation movements of Germany and Switzerland. (We've encountered him before as leader of the Schmalkaldic League.) Since Zwingli and Luther had never met but had much in common, Philip encouraged the two men to meet in person to see if their movements could be unified as one. The primary doctrine that separated them was the Lord's Supper. As mentioned, Luther believed that the elements were the actual body and blood of Christ after consecration; Zwingli, in turn, believed that they were merely symbolic, only representing the body and blood of Christ.

Zwingli traveled by boat on the Rhine, Luther traveled from Wittenberg by horse and wagon, and the two met at Marburg (north of modern Frankfurt). A spirited discussion was inevitable. Zwingli argued that Christ's body could not possibly be present in the Lord's Supper because He spoke the words "This is my body" while He was still in His earthly body. And Christ could not be mystically present because His mystical body is the church, which is not referred to as being delivered unto death. By process of elimination, Zwingli concluded that the elements were symbolic only.

In reply, Luther had written a pamphlet in which he expounded his view of the real presence of Christ in the sacrament. He held that "each of Christ's natures permeates the other, and His humanity participates in the attributes of His divinity." If God is omnipresent, Luther argued, just so the body and blood of Christ is omnipresent and possible in the sacrament. He wanted the words of Christ to be taken literally, though he denied there was a change in the substances.

The Famous Debate

Luther came to the debate already prejudiced against the Swiss because, in his mind, they were radicals like Carlstadt had been in Wittenberg. The smashing of images, the rejection of musical instruments, and church services without liturgy made him wary of Zwingli and his delegation.

Here are a few excerpts from their debate about the Lord's Supper. Luther thundered,

> Your basic contentions are these: In the last analysis you wish to prove that a body cannot be at two places at once. . . . I do not question how Christ can be God and man and how the two natures can be joined. For God is more powerful than all our ideas, and we must submit to his Word. Prove that Christ's body is not there where the Scripture says, "This is my body." Rational proofs I will not listen to. Corporeal proofs, arguments based on geometrical principles I repudiate absolutely. . . . God is beyond all mathematics, and the words of God are to be revered and carried out in awe. It is God who commands, "Take, eat, this is my body." I request, therefore, valid scriptural proof to the contrary.

At this point, Luther wrote the words "This is my body" on the table in chalk and covered it with a velvet cloth.

Zwingli countered,

> It is prejudice, a preconception, which keeps Doctor Luther from yielding his point. He refuses to yield until a passage is quoted that proves that the body in the Lord's Supper is figurative. . . . Comparison of scriptural passages is always necessary. Although we have no scriptural passage that says, "this is the sign of the body," we still have proof that Christ dismissed the idea of a physical repast [meal] . . . in John 6 [Christ] moves away from the idea of a physical repast. . . . From this it follows that Christ did not give himself in the Lord's Supper in a physical sense. . . . You yourself have acknowledged that it is the spiritual repast that offers solace. And

since we are agreed on this major question, I beg you for the love of Christ not to burden anyone with the crime of heresy because of these differences.[6]

Zwingli then demonstrated from Scripture that some statements are symbolic. He argued that Luther was simply refusing

Luther and Zwingli never agreed about the nature of the Lord's Supper.

to recognize a figure of speech. But at the end of the debate, Luther stoutly maintained his belief in the real presence, or consubstantiation. He felt that to deny this doctrine would lead to accepting other heresies. Zwingli remained unshaken in his memorial view, comparing the sacrament to a wedding ring that seals the marriage union between Christ and the believer.

No minds were changed in those ten days. The Swiss, however, extended the hand of fellowship to acknowledge the Lutherans as their Christian brothers. Luther appeared willing to agree, but Philipp Melanchthon reminded him that if they were to show unity with the Swiss radicals, there would be no possibility of future reconciliation with the Catholics. Thus Luther did not shake Zwingli's hand. In his mind, they were not really brothers in Christ, not just because Zwingli denied the real presence of Christ in the sacrament but because Zwingli, unlike Luther, believed it was proper for Protestants to fight when being attacked by Catholic armies. Luther was not a pacifist, but he believed that only the magistrate could go to war; the state could declare war, but if Christians were attacked they were not to fight with swords but to get on their knees. In his mind, the Swiss were too radical, and in some critical matters, they were also wrong.

Because of the tenacity of both sides, the division remained, as is evident even today between Lutheran and Reformed churches. Philip of Hesse's vision of a united Reformed Church was never realized.

Zwingli's Death

Zwingli went home from his debate with Luther at a time when tensions between Catholics and Protestants were escalating. When economic sanctions were enacted against the Catholics, 8,000 Catholic soldiers advanced on Zurich; the Protestants, on such short notice, could recruit only about 1,500 men and would have to wait until reinforcements could arrive. Zwingli went out with the soldiers not just as a chaplain but with sword and helmet. Bainton writes, "Here was the crusader, the priest in arms, the leader of an elect people, like Gideon of Israel."[7] Elect or not, the forces of Zurich were routed. Zwingli was captured along with other leaders. His body was quartered by the executioner and the ashes thrown to the wind. Luther regarded his death as a judgment for having taken the sword on behalf of the gospel.

What followed was a peace that allowed the reform movement in Switzerland to keep its gains but not spread. Catholic minorities could live peaceably in Protestant areas, but once again, Protestant minorities were not tolerated in Catholic lands. However, the medieval belief in one God, one faith, and one baptism in one country had forever disappeared.

14

The Anabaptists

Promise and Persecution

On several occasions over the years, I've led tour groups to the banks of the Limmat River in Zurich to the place where several Anabaptists were forcibly drowned with Huldrych Zwingli's tacit approval. Among them was one of his personal disciples, Felix Manz. This is a story that must be told; it is not only a story of courage on the part of this young disciple but it also highlights the controversy that swirled in Zwingli's day about the much-debated question: *What is the church?*

The three most famous reformers, Luther, Calvin, and Zwingli, had, in my opinion, contradictory views of the church. On the one hand, they knew that people within their congregations were converted through personal faith in Christ. On the other hand, they thought of the church as regional, encompassing all who were born within the boundaries of the Holy Roman Empire. They were insistent that the medieval vision

Opponents drowned Anabaptists as an ironic punishment.

of a unified Christendom remain in place to give cohesion to society and to inculcate Christian values. Thus they held strongly to a Christianized Europe that developed after Constantine, who, after his own conversion to Christianity, appointed Christian bishops and tried to use religion to unite his empire.

Nothing so symbolized the continuation of a unified Christendom than infant baptism, which "guaranteed" that all who were born into European society would be a part of the larger regional church. Infant baptism was practiced at least since the time of Cyprian of North Africa, but after the time of Constantine, the practice spread to all of Europe as the various countries embraced the idea of a regional, unified Christianized society.

Memorial plate beside the Limmat River in remembrance of Felix Manz and other martyred Anabaptists.

Thanks to Zwingli's genius, he attracted a group of young men who were interested in learning Greek and the classics. Among them was a youthful scholar named Conrad Grebel, and they were later joined by Felix Manz. However, by 1523, these young men had lost confidence in Zwingli because he refused to set the church free from its entanglement with the state. They believed that Zwingli should not be beholden to the town council, to which he looked to settle church matters.

In their opinion, Zwingli had betrayed his vow that he would not compromise where the Word of God had spoken. In the word of one historian, "The decision of Conrad Grebel to refuse to accept the jurisdiction of the Zurich council over the Zurich church is one of the high moments of history, for however obscure it was, it marked the beginning of the modern 'free church' movement."[1]

Zwingli's young disciples couldn't find infant baptism anywhere in the New Testament, yet it was mandated by both church and state. A pastor who preached against it was imprisoned. (Interestingly, Zwingli himself had preached against infant baptism at one point, but later said he had been mistaken.)

The Beginning of the Free Church in Switzerland

Then it happened. On January 21, 1525, about a dozen men trudged through the snow to enter the home of Felix Manz near the Grossmünster Church, prepared to baptize one another. In fear they bowed their heads as they went to their knees praying that God might show them His will and grant them courage. After the prayer, they baptized one another and pledged themselves to be disciples of Christ, no matter the cost.

Thus, Anabaptism, the "*re*baptizer" movement, was born. The men had been baptized as infants, but now they were baptized as adults on the profession of their personal faith in Christ. No other event so completely symbolized a break with Rome. "Here, for the first time in the course of the Reformation, a group of Christians dared to form a church after what was conceived to be the New Testament pattern."[2]

Their church was free from the state and free from the traditions of Rome. They believed that the state couldn't be "Christianized," even if the emperor changed his religion to Christianity. The world, they argued, remains the world, and if the church wasn't persecuted, it was because the "salt has lost its savor"—the light had gone out. The church had to walk down a different path; it must always be at war with the world with its values and worldly leadership and expect persecution from the state.

The first Anabaptist martyr was Eberli Bolt, a preacher who was burned at the stake at the hands of Roman Catholic authorities on May 29, 1525. As for Zwingli's disciple Conrad Grebel, he was an Anabaptist preacher for only twenty months. He went from house to house witnessing, baptizing, and conducting the Lord's Supper. On one occasion, he baptized five hundred converts in the Sitter River. He

The Grossmünster (left) and the Wasserkirche on the banks of the Limmat River in Zurich

was finally arrested and thrown into the castle prison at Grüningen; he later died of the plague. Three weeks later another friend, Felix Manz, was also incarcerated and awaited his cruel fate.

To put it clearly, the Anabaptists were a threat to the medieval order that united the church and the state. By baptizing only those who professed faith in Christ, they affirmed that the church was a minority within society; by no means should the church be identified with the totality of society. Christianity, they insisted, demanded a lifestyle that could be achieved only by the redeemed, not by those who believe they are Christians because they were baptized as infants.

The Anabaptists insisted that a child could not be made a Christian even if an ocean of water were poured on his or her head. They said that infant baptism is therefore no baptism at all but "a dipping in a Romish bath." Consequently, these "radicals" objected to being called Anabaptists; they were not *re*baptizers, they argued, because when they had water sprinkled on their heads as infants, they weren't really baptized at all. They believed that God, by the Word and Spirit, worked directly in the heart of those who believe in Christ, giving them the gift of the Holy Spirit and power to live a new life. Only such people were worthy of baptism.

Zurich, they contended, was an unweeded field that could not possibly be considered as the "New Israel" of God; since wheat and tares grew together, there must be a purging if the true believers were to form God-honoring churches. God would make the final separation, but believers are commanded to keep the church as pure as they can through discipline and watchful obedience.

The church and state should therefore separate since the state is concerned with everyone in the community, whereas the church consists only of the saints. In fact, many Anabaptists took the next step by insisting that the true believer should have nothing to do with the state. The state, they said, had been ordained by God because of sin and is therefore best left for sinners to manage. Thus they withdrew from political life. They repudiated war, capital punishment, and the courts. They also refused to lift a sword in self-defense and refused to make oaths since, they said, Christ forbade it. They were sheep among wolves, and if the Good Shepherd did not protect them, they would follow him to death—even as sheep to the slaughter.

This didn't necessarily mean that Anabaptists were rebellious citizens. Indeed, most of them were committed to obeying the laws of the state as long as the laws didn't conflict with their religious practices.

Every member of their flock was regarded as a missionary. Men and women left their homes to go on evangelistic tours where multitudes were converted to the faith as they believed it. In some of the communities in Switzerland and in the Rhine Valley, the Anabaptists began to outnumber the Protestants and Catholics combined.[3]

They called for a life of strict morality and, by the grace of God, many achieved it. Zwingli said of them, "At first contact their conduct appears irreproachable, pious, unassuming, attractive. . . . Even those who are inclined to be critical will say that their lives are excellent."[4] And if further proof is needed, a Catholic observed in them "no lying, deception, swearing, strife, harsh language, no intemperate eating and drinking, no outward personal display, but rather humility, patience, uprightness, meekness, honesty, temperance, straightforwardness in such a measure that one would suppose that they had the Holy Spirit of God."[5]

That is high praise.

One would think that the Reformers would be glad to have such examples of Christian conduct. But the opposite was the case. The Reformers turned against them, believing that their radical separation from the state, as evidenced by believer's baptism, was destroying the fabric of Christendom. Obviously, the conviction of nonresistance troubled the authorities. After all, who would go to war with the Turks if pacifism were widely accepted?

These radicals needed harsh treatment.

The Martyrdom of the Anabaptists

This commitment to a unified Christendom was strongly affirmed at the Diet of Speyer in Germany in 1529. Although the Protestants were given some freedoms, both Catholics and Protestants agreed that those who practiced believer's baptism should be put to death by fire, drowning, or sword. We shouldn't be surprised that the same penalty was enacted in Switzerland. On March 7, 1526, the Zurich city council decreed "that no one in town, country, and domain, whether man, woman, or girl shall henceforth baptize another. Whoever hereafter baptizes someone will be apprehended by our Lords and, according to this present decree, be drowned without mercy."[6]

The first victim of this decree was Zwingli's former friend, Felix Manz, who was taken six hundred yards from the town hall in Zurich and led to a boat. His hands and feet were bound, and then he was pushed into the water with the voice of his mother and brother above the waves, urging him to remain true to the faith. His last words were, "Into thy hands, O Lord, I commend my spirit." With that he disappeared under the cold dark waters of the Limmat River a half-mile from the Grossmünster.

As for Zwingli, it is said he was on the shore, and with more than a touch of sarcasm said, "If he wishes to go under the water, let him go under." In other words, if Manz wants to be baptized, let us baptize him by drowning him! This began unbelievable persecution against the Anabaptists. (My friend Timothy George, who wrote an excellent book on the theology of the Reformers, told me that *more Anabaptist Christians were martyred after the Reformation than Christians who died in the early persecutions of Rome!*)

Roland Bainton says that one only has to examine an Anabaptist hymnbook and read their names with the notations, "Drowned 1525, burned 1526, beheaded 1527, hanged 1528, and so on."[7] Sometimes whole congregations were killed at once, or the leader was taken and forced to dig his own grave. After recording the deaths of 2,173 of the brethren, one chronicler writes,

> No human being was able to take away out of their hearts what they had experienced. . . . The fire of God burned within them. They would die ten deaths rather than forsake the divine truth. They had drunk of the water which is flowing from God's sanctuary, yea the water of life. Their tent they had pitched not here upon earth, but in eternity. Their faith blossomed like a lily, their loyalty as a rose, their piety and candor as the flower of the garden of God. The angel of the Lord battled for them that they could not be deprived of the helmet of salvation. Therefore they have borne all torture and agony without fear. The things of this world they counted only as shadows. They were thus drawn unto God that they knew nothing, sought nothing, desired nothing, loved nothing but God alone. Therefore they had more patience in their suffering than their enemies in tormenting them.[8]

We are humbled at their simple, God-directed devotion.

The Lunatic Fringe

For ten years the Anabaptist movement was without offense. Though hunted, burned, beheaded, and drowned, they, for the most part, remained true to the faith. But thanks to a lunatic fringe, the image of Anabaptists would be tarnished and their movement blemished.

In 1534, some radical Anabaptists selected the town of Münster in Westphalia as the New Jerusalem. These reckless fanatics violated their commitment to pacifism and violently took over the local town government. They marched into the town square as sheep to be slaughtered but carried swords just in case they chose to fight. A "revelation of the Spirit" was received, and the fight began.

In their zeal they tried to imitate the patriarchs and prophets as well as the apostles. Some followed the prophet Isaiah, who was instructed by God to walk naked; another, also following Isaiah, took a hot coal to his lips. Polygamy was introduced after the example of the Abraham, Isaac, and Jacob. To end the madness, Catholics and Lutherans joined forces to recapture the "New City of Jerusalem"—the town was taken and the leaders killed by the sword.

Unfortunately, in the minds of many, Anabaptists were henceforth identified with the excesses of this lunatic fringe. The event cast a long shadow over the more sober commitment of tens of thousands who stood true to the faith, shunning the lunacy of the Münster radicals.

The Birth of the Mennonites

Menno Simons, the founder of the Mennonites, and Jacob Hutter, founder of the Hutterites, repudiated the actions of the Münster radicals. These

Menno Simons advocated pacifism, which distanced him and his followers from the "madmen of Münster."

pious Anabaptists urged their followers to return to the basic pattern of the New Testament: simplicity, sobriety, poverty, and meekness. The true Christian must crucify the flesh and live a life that is "void of offense before God and men." Women must wear no costly jewelry, swords must be beaten into plowshares, and love must be extended to enemies. Yet for all this, persecution against them continued. Only God knows the true number of the thousands who were cruelly massacred.

This is not the place to debate the complexity of the question of what the relationship between the church and the state should be. The problem has divided Christians for centuries. Regardless, we must admire the Anabaptists for their devotion to Christ and their unwavering commitment to their vision of a pure church not entangled with the world.

15

Calvin

Reforming Geneva

I f you do not stay in Geneva, you will be cursed!"

With these words, the fiery preacher Guillaume Farel addressed John Calvin when the young scholar visited Geneva in 1536. Calvin had gone to Geneva to escape the persecution of Protestants in France, and when he arrived, he was surprised that the people there had heard of him. Now he stood face to face with its most prominent Protestant leader, who was trying to persuade him to stay in Geneva to help the fledgling reform movement that had begun in the city several years earlier.

In the room of a Geneva inn, Farel listened to Calvin give numerous reasons why he shouldn't lead the Reformation in Geneva. Calvin argued that his youth, inexperience, and temperament were not suited for the turbulence that such responsibilities would bring. Then the old man rose from his chair, directed his piercing gaze squarely into Calvin's eyes, pointed his finger at him, and said, "May God curse your studies if now in her time of need you refuse to lend your aid to His church!" Calvin relented, moved to Geneva, and would become a "second generation" reformer.

St. Peter's Cathedral, Geneva

Keep in mind that by this time it had been nineteen years since Luther had nailed his *Ninety-Five Theses* to the Castle Church door in Wittenberg. His books, pamphlets, and ideas had found their way well beyond the borders of Germany. Thus, many people in Switzerland were turning to Protestantism, and leaders for the movement were desperately needed.

As for Farel, he had come to Geneva in 1532 to strengthen the Reformation movement that had already begun. He was a persuasive preacher who convinced many of the citizens of Geneva to turn to the Protestant faith. He was able to capture St. Peter's Cathedral (in French, St. Pierre), Geneva's largest and most famous church. Its images were destroyed, the mass abolished, and the monks driven out. On May 21, 1536, the general assembly of the city voted in favor of the Reformation, and Protestantism became the official religion of the city. But Farel knew that he was too old to give leadership to the struggling Protestant movement, and he went about persuading Calvin to take over.

How had Farel become aware of John Calvin? Calvin's textbook on Reformed theology, *Institutes of the Christian Religion*, had made him known throughout Europe—and to Farel. Calvin was only twenty-seven years old when the first edition was published. Though it would later be revised and expanded, this book would serve as a theological primer that would have a great influence in Europe for two hundred years. Today, millions of people still read the *Institutes*.

In his book, Calvin set forth a view of God, man, and the church that would inspire millions to Christian service and commitment. Calvin believed that the fall of humanity into sin was so pervasive and affected people's minds and wills so much that they couldn't believe the truths of the gospel unless God were to perform a miracle of regeneration in their hearts. Because God's purposes can never be thwarted, it was exactly such a miracle that God performed in the hearts of His elect. This belief in predestination was to become the doctrine for which Calvin would be best known. We will return to this in a moment.

Calvin's Story

John Calvin was a beneficiary of God's special grace. He was born in northern France in 1509 and studied for a brief time at the University of Paris, where he was introduced to the writings of Martin Luther. After Calvin finished his humanistic studies, his father sent him to the University of Orléans in France to study law; he transferred to the University of Bourges in 1529.

Calvin tells us very little about his own conversion but explains that he was addicted to the superstitions of the papacy and that nothing less than an act of God could have extricated him from those beliefs. He says that God turned his course in a different direction by the hidden bridle of His providence. "My mind . . . , despite my youth, had been hardened. . . . By a sudden conversion God turned and brought it to docility."[1] God, he said, tamed his mind and overcame his darkness, resulting in his conversion. No doubt it was the writings of Luther, whose ideas had spread to the universities of France and Switzerland, that brought the light of the gospel to his mind. Although the two reformers never met, they read each other's writings with appreciation. Calvin called Luther his "most respected father."

Persecution in France

Even as Calvin was finishing his formal studies, persecution of Protestants in France had already begun. In October 1534, Protestants anonymously placed placards in prominent locations throughout France that vigorously denounced the Catholic mass. King Francis I awoke that morning to discover one of these signs outside his bedchamber. He was both fearful and angry. His anger sparked the vigorous persecution of Protestants that continued until the Edict of Nantes in 1598. Hundreds of Protestants were imprisoned, and thirty-five were burned at the stake, including some of Calvin's close friends.

This crisis motivated Calvin to write *Institutes of the Christian Religion*. He wanted King Francis (to whom the book was dedicated) to understand Protestantism, and to prove that it was not to be confused with the excesses of the Anabaptists. He was convinced that those who read his writings would better grasp the rational and biblical basis for the Protestant faith.

As we have learned, in Switzerland, the city council voted on which religion it would follow; when Catholics were dominant, Protestants were persecuted; when Protestants were in charge, they persecuted the Catholics. Calvin insisted that the forms of worship and doctrine should be determined by church leaders, not the civil authorities that controlled matters related to the city. But he was overruled and so fled to Strasbourg, France, for three years. There he continued his studies and married Idelette van Buren, a woman from the southern Netherlands. He also revised his *Institutes* and became acquainted with other leaders of the Reformation movement.

When Calvin was away from Geneva, Cardinal Sadoleto wrote a reasoned letter to the people of Geneva explaining why they should return to the Catholic Church. Calvin, who became aware of the letter, with no less polish, wrote a brilliant reply. Within time, those who were opposed to Calvin lost in the city elections, and Calvin was invited back. He returned on September 13, 1541.

The Church

Once reestablished in Geneva, Calvin attempted to make the city the New Israel of God, reminiscent of what Zwingli had done in Zurich. Calvin believed that, like ancient Israel, the city should make a covenant with God to worship the Lord alone and stand against the seductions of Babylon. There were penalties for fortune telling, making noise in church, or betting on Sunday. Taverns were abolished, and church attendance was mandatory. A goldsmith might be punished for making a chalice for a Catholic priest, or parents might be admonished if they named their children after one of the Catholic saints.

Catholics were permitted to stay in Geneva if they remained quiet; however, they were eliminated from government and urged to convert and mend their ways. Geneva was becoming a select city, as one might expect from a city that was "the Israel of God." Like Zwingli, Calvin embraced the concept of a regional church but at the same time held that the true church was limited to a small group within the larger sphere of Christendom. In other words, everyone in Geneva belonged to the wider church, but only those who sought God and had the assurance of their salvation belonged to the true church of the elect.

Persecution in other European countries inspired many Christian refugees to flood into Geneva from the 1540s into the seventeenth century. As many as six thousand people came to escape persecution and live in a city that had a population of thirteen thousand. Thus Geneva was becoming known as a magnet for "elect" saints. When the refugees

John Calvin

returned to their homelands, they took the teachings of Calvin with them, thereby spreading Calvinism to England, Scotland, the Netherlands, and eventually to the New World.

The Burning of Servetus

Ask any person who has even a smattering of knowledge about Calvin, and they'll mention two things: the doctrine of predestination and the burning of Michael Servetus at the stake. For these transgressions, Voltaire believed that Calvin was in the lowest parts of hell. However, some of us might object to such a harsh evaluation.

Here's the story. Servetus was a brilliant, educated Spanish physician who simply was unable to accept the doctrine of the Trinity. Catholic authorities in France had convicted him, but he escaped from prison in Vienne (a commune in southern France) and then fled to Geneva, thinking that Calvin would give him refuge. Catholic authorities sought his extradition to face charges of heresy.

Thus, Calvin had to deal with this heretic who came to live in the city. Calvin would eventually be blamed for putting Servetus to death, but we must put this event in perspective. First, the condemnation and execution of Servetus was the work of the city council of Geneva. Though they were the ones to condemn Servetus, Calvin cooperated by laying out the charges against the heretic.

Calvin spent many hours with Servetus trying to persuade him to change his beliefs. When the council voted for

In addition to his part in Calvin's story, Servetus is highly regarded in many fields as an innovative humanist and scientist.

Monument in honor of Michael Servetus

the death penalty, Calvin suggested that he be beheaded, believing that such a death was less painful than being burned at the stake. His suggestion was refused, and Servetus was burned as a heretic on October 27, 1553.

We have every right to protest against the cruelty of earlier generations; freedom of religion is a cardinal doctrine for us and generally accepted as universally desirable. What we do not have the right to do is to single out Calvin as a mean Protestant who had a man executed because of a doctrinal error. The fact is that throughout Europe, Catholics and Protestants persecuted and often killed those who were regarded as heretics. We can't criticize Calvin unless we also mention the persecution of the Protestants in France and later events such as the Spanish Inquisition.

Many years ago on a tour of Geneva, I took the time to find the place where Servetus was burned at the stake. Today there's a monument at a busy intersection that marks the spot. In its reference to the event, it correctly notes that "Calvin was a son of his times." And so he was.

Predestination

But Calvin is best known to many of us because of his theological teachings about God, redemption, and the doctrine of providence. Calvin's doctrines regarding predestination grew out of pastoral concerns. He knew that his people needed comfort in very difficult times, and they needed to understand the doctrine of God and His ways in the world. Though Calvin was very pessimistic about the nature of humanity, he was optimistic about the purposes of God. He wrote, "In the very darkness that frightens [many people] appears not only the usefulness of this teaching, but its very sweet fruit."[2]

Calvin began by contemplating why some people are saved and others are lost. As he studied the Scriptures, he learned that all of us are equally dead in trespasses and sins; we are, by nature, the children of wrath, and no one seeks after God. In order for a person to be saved, God must grant life to the dead corpse; God must overcome the blindness of the human heart and do what we cannot do.

Therefore, the reason some believe and others don't isn't found in us (for we are all equally blind and dead); it must be found in God. Those whom the Almighty chooses are quickened by Him and granted the gift of eternal life.

Though Calvin, to my knowledge, did not use this illustration, I think he would have approved of it. When Christ went to the tomb of Lazarus, He didn't ask Lazarus whether he wanted to be raised, because the dead are quite unable to make decisions such as that. Jesus had to make the decision for Lazarus and give the command for him to be resurrected. Just so, Jesus said, "For as the Father raises the dead and gives them life, so also the Son gives life to whom he will" (John 5:21). Of course, in the case of the physically dead, they are not involved in any facet of their resurrection. In the case of the spiritually dead, they do exercise faith, but only because God gives them life and enables them to believe. In both cases, it's God who makes the decision to raise them from their death.

Rightly understood, this doctrine of predestination is the basis of security. It brings "no shaking of the faith but rather faith's confirmation." To be assured of one's election is to be motivated to press on with perseverence. The doctrine also stirs zeal for evangelism. Since we don't know who belongs to the company of the elect, we should urge all people to be saved. We are confident that God can raise the vilest sinner if He so chooses.

Calvin is not the one who coined the idea of presenting his theology of salvation in "five points." But when a man named Arminius objected to Calvin's doctrine of predestination and its implications, he and his followers drafted five objections to Calvinism. The Synod of Dort was convened in the Netherlands in 1618 to respond to the Arminian challenge. The synod adopted and defended what today we call the five pillars of Calvinism (sometimes remembered by the acrostic TULIP). Below is a brief summary of the five points of the Calvinistic doctrine of salvation.

The Famous Five Points: TULIP

Total Depravity

"Total depravity" simply means that we inherit the guilt of Adam's sin (Rom. 5:12) and are by nature children of wrath (Eph. 2:3). The corruption of sin extends to the mind and the will; consequently, no one can seek God on his or her own. God must draw people to Himself, regenerate them, and give them faith to believe the gospel.

While others might merely say that humanity was sick, Calvin believed humanity was dead. If we were only sick, common grace might help us recover by enabling us to make a right choice. But if we are spiritually dead, we need the Giver of Life to take the initiative in salvation.

Unconditional Election

Based on the doctrine of total depravity and the teaching of Scripture, some people are saved because God elected them unconditionally to have eternal life (John 15:16; Acts 13:48; Eph. 1:4; 2 Thess. 2:13). Others whom God has not chosen are eternally lost. Calvin took no delight in the fact that not all were saved; indeed, he struggled and grieved over God's decree, but he believed it because the Scriptures clearly taught it.

Limited Atonement

"Limited atonement" simply means that Christ did not die for all people in general but gave Himself only for the true church—the elect. Calvinists tell us that this doctrine is necessary to preserve the two basic attributes of God: His justice and the integrity of His purposes. The point is this: If Jesus paid for everyone's sin, should not everyone be forgiven by God since God's requirements have been justly met? If the treachery of Judas was included in Christ's ransom, which was accepted by the Father, why should Judas be required to suffer for his sins?

In other words, the doctrine of limited atonement (or as it should be called, *particular* atonement) teaches that Jesus actually got what He paid for. Verses to support this theory of the atonement are numerous. Isaiah 53:5 says that Christ was wounded for "our transgressions." Husbands are to love their wives just "as Christ loved the church and gave himself up *for her*" (Eph. 5:25, emphasis mine).

A strong objection is often raised to this doctrine based on 1 John 2:2, where we read that Christ is "the propitiation for our sins, and not for ours only but also for the sins of the whole world." Calvinists respond by saying that the expression "whole world" is sometimes used in Scripture as a reference to all in a certain class, not necessarily each individual. Christ, for example, said He would "draw all people" to himself (John 12:32). This certainly did not mean every individual would be drawn to Christ, for relatively few are drawn to Christ in comparison to the perishing multitudes.

However, most Calvinists would say that Christ's death was sufficient for the sins of the whole world but is *efficient* only for the elect. In that sense, Christ's death was for the whole world, but God applies these benefits only to the elect. The intention of the one payment on the cross was to redeem a people for God that Jesus frequently referred to as "those You have given me" (John 17:24 HCSB).

Irresistible Grace

"Irresistible grace" can be a very confusing doctrine if it is not properly defined. Of course there are verses of Scripture that clearly teach that the Holy Spirit can be resisted. For example, Stephen, as he was being stoned, accused his fellow Jews of resisting the Holy Spirit (Acts 7:51). But Calvinists believe that the elect cannot continually resist the Holy Spirit in the matter of salvation. They will eventually respond as the Holy Spirit draws them to Christ. This is irresistible grace, or it could more properly be called "effectual grace"—grace that accomplishes its work in the lives of those whom God chooses.

Perseverance of the Saints

The "perseverance of the saints" is the logical outcome of the preceding doctrines. It means that the elect will persevere in their faith and none will be lost. Christ affirmed, "All that the Father gives me will come to me. . . . And this is the will of him who sent me, that I should lose nothing of all that he has given me, but raise it up on the last day" (John 6:37, 39).

A wooden chair in St. Peter's Cathedral used by Calvin

The doctrines of Calvinism have been debated for centuries. The most common objection to the above doctrines is that election, as understood by Calvinists, turns people into puppets: if you are elect, God will cause you to believe; if not, you will be damned because you cannot believe the gospel.

Space forbids a detailed response to all these issues. Here I wish only to point out that Calvinists affirm that God does not bypass the human will but works in and through the human will to give the elect the disposition to believe the gospel. Thus, the elect accept the gospel voluntarily because God has so worked in their hearts that they have the willingness to believe. God works through the human will and not independent of it.[3]

Like him or hate him, none can deny that Calvin's impact has continued for the last five hundred years. While Martin Luther's influence was largely confined to Germany, John Calvin was a reformer of several countries of Europe. The historian William Stevenson writes, "Left to itself, Lutheranism might well have foundered: it required Calvinism to keep the Reformed ship afloat. And in the world as a whole we may also remember Calvin as the greatest religious force in modern times."[4]

Calvin died in 1568 and did not want a marker on his grave for the simple reason that he did not want to have his followers venerate him as the Catholics do their departed saints. However, the approximate location of his burial is memorialized in a Geneva cemetery.

16

Calvinism's Lasting Influence

John Calvin was not universally loved. When his hometown of Noyon, France, received the news of his death in 1551, the people celebrated and gave thanks to God for taking this heretic from their midst. As it turned out, their rejoicing was cut short because the rumor of his death was premature. They still had thirteen more years to put up with this "heretic."[1]

Throughout the centuries, Calvin has been variously admired and hated. But even today, his foes must grudgingly admit that his impact has been both great and lasting throughout Europe and the United States. Millions of Christians who disagree with Calvin's view of the church nevertheless gladly embrace the Reformed doctrine of salvation and Calvin's emphasis on God's sovereignty in individual lives and world affairs. His grand view of God's greatness and providence has survived in the minds and hearts of many for five hundred years.

Whereas Luther founded the one formal Lutheran Church, Calvin's influence created the French Huguenot Church, the Scottish Presbyterian

Church, the Dutch Reformed Church, and the English Puritans. Due to persecution, the Huguenot Church in Calvin's homeland of France did not survive, nor did it have a lasting influence there. But its story must be told.

The French Huguenots

Although the Reformation in France was at first greatly influenced by Luther, Calvin soon surpassed the impact of the German Reformer. After all, Calvin was a Frenchman; *Institutes of the Christian Religion* was written in excellent French, thereby giving the people a theological basis for their convictions written in their own language. Calvin's influence grew because he trained pastors in Geneva who went to France to spread the Reformed faith. He also carried on regular correspondence with the Protestant leaders in France, giving them both advice and encouragement. In one of his letters to a young pastor who was suffering under persecution, Calvin tenderly wrote, "I wish I could trade places with you so that what you are enduring would fall upon me." Gradually, small groups of Protestants met secretly throughout France for Bible study and prayer. Many of these small groups formed into churches.

Persecution only drove them underground, where they waited to emerge when conditions became more favorable. William Stevenson writes, "Protestantism was entrenched in every district in France and was especially strong in the towns, along the great waterways and rivers, and in those areas that lay at a distance from Paris or were accessible to foreign influence."[2] In fact, in some areas, Protestants were actually in the majority. Around 1552, this group was given the name "Huguenots," whose meaning is obscure. Among this group of Protestants were people involved in commerce, those from the lower professional classes, and a few of the nobility. The most famous French name associated with this Protestant cause was Gaspard de Coligny (1519–72), admiral in the French military.

In August of 1562, a royal declaration demanded that the citizens of France adhere to the Catholic rites alone, and many so-called Huguenots crumbled under the pressure, rebaptizing their children into the Catholic faith. Meanwhile, the faithful continued to die. However, the Protestant movement was preserved despite the stiff and targeted opposition.

This resilience of the Protestant faith was a threat to the Catholic leadership, and in order to stem the tide, Catherine de Medici instigated the St. Bartholomew's Day Massacre in 1572. The massacre began the eve of the feast of St. Bartholomew the Apostle. The military and political leader of the Huguenots, Gaspard de Coligny, was assassinated, and soon after a slaughter directed against the Huguenots spread throughout Paris. Lasting several weeks, it expanded to other French cities and towns. Modern estimates for the number of Protestant dead across France vary widely from five thousand to thirty thousand.

Historians estimate that between five thousand and thirty thousand French Protestants were massacred by Catholics in just a few weeks in 1572.

Although the Huguenot movement was crippled by the loss of so many of its leaders and ran-and-file followers, it was not completely crushed. The Protestants continued in their quest for equal acceptance with the Catholic majority. And in April of 1598, King Henry IV of France granted them substantial rights with the signing of the Edict of Nantes, which opened the path to tolerance and freedom of conscience.

However, nearly eighty-seven years later, in October of 1685, King Louis XIV revoked the treaty, insisting that a country cannot be under one law and one king unless it was also under one religious system. Like most leaders before him, he believed that political unity demanded religious conformity.

Louis declared that all concessions that had been earlier ratified were to be withdrawn, and "in consequence we desire . . . that all the temples of the people of the aforesaid so-called Reformed religion . . . should be demolished forthwith." Freedom of assembly was abolished, and those who would not embrace the Catholic faith were told "to depart from our kingdom and the lands subject to us within fifteen days from the publication of our present edict . . . on pain of the galleys."[3] The edict went on to say that when these people left France they couldn't take any possessions with them. All children born within the borders of France were required to be baptized in the Catholic faith.

With that, Louis now launched a methodical governmental campaign against the Huguenots in a determined effort to religiously unify France. He hounded them out of public life, banned them from government office, and excluded them from professions such as printing and medicine. Thus, the Protestants didn't gain equal rights in France until the French Revolution.

To escape persecution, tens of thousands of Huguenots left the country (perhaps as many as two hundred thousand) and found refuge in other lands such as Prussia, Holland, England, the United States, and others. This was a catastrophe for France since it lost so many productive citizens, but it was a boon to the countries that received them. Thus the Huguenots contributed to Protestantism in all these countries.

The Scottish Presbyterian Church

In Scotland, one of Calvin's disciples, John Knox, almost singlehandedly wove Calvinism into the fabric of Scottish Christianity. Knox spent two years with Calvin in Geneva and would return to Scotland with a passion to spread the gospel he had come to love.

Knox, believed to have been the descendant of agricultural peasants and born in the early 1500s, was unimposing with his short frame, but he was fearsome with his speech. We know little about his turn to Protestantism, but he was probably confronted by Luther's works along with the Word of God while attending the University of St. Andrews. He was impulsive, brash, and often unkind; in the conflict between Protestantism and Catholicism in Scotland, he unabashedly declared the mass to be idolatry and prayers to Mary pagan. He was zealous for holy worship.

Knox had come to love Calvin and the city of Geneva, which he deemed to be "the most perfect school of Christ." He appreciated the discipline and purity of the city and longed to re-create such cities in Scotland. But how could this be accomplished with the Roman Catholics occupying the positions of power?

Protestantism in Scotland was gaining momentum, and in 1559, a revolution pushed out the French Catholic influence. The churches were quickly transformed into Reformed enclaves,

Statue of John Knox at New College, Edinburgh, Scotland

with images, which they considered idolatrous, removed in exchange for the prominence of preaching the Word of God. Thus, what we know today as Scottish Presbyterianism was born, and within time, Scotland became the most Calvinistic country in existence.

Knox not only had an impact in Scotland, but he also had returned to England in 1549 and urged the Anglican Church to abandon some of the rituals and practices held over from Catholicism and accept the doctrine and practices of the Reformed faith. As such, some historians would say Knox was the founder of the Puritan movement.

With a full and laborious life, he continued to preach, even being carried to the pulpit in his final days. Knox died in 1572 not knowing that millions of Christians around the world in South Korea, Africa, and the United States would call themselves Presbyterians and, to a greater or lesser degree, continue to follow Calvinist teachings.

England and the Puritans

In England, the reforms that began under Henry VIII resulted in the development of the Church of England, or Anglicanism. This transformation involved the acceptance of Protestant theology but the retention of much of the liturgy of Catholicism.

However, when Calvinism gained a foothold in England, its followers became known as Puritans because they insisted that other Anglicans simply didn't go far enough in their reforms. These Puritans tried to influence the Anglican Church to purify itself by ending its halfway reforms and become completely "Reformed." They believed that the Anglicans had never truly shaken the dust of Rome from their feet.

Numerous English towns employed lecturers who would offer popular weekday sermons outside Anglican liturgical constraints. Many Puritans who had studied at Cambridge and other colleges filled these positions. But we must mention that the preaching alone did not win their hearers. The dramatic holiness of the Puritans, living out their teachings as a consistent example, buoyed the growth of the movement.

A second generation ushered in the peak of Puritanism during the middle of the 1600s. John Owen, Richard Baxter, John Bunyan (the author of *Pilgrim's Progress*), John Flavel, and William Gouge are some of the more famous ministers of the age. This ascendency was forged in tragedy as the Puritans faced substantial persecution in the 1630s under the wrath of the Anglican archbishop William Laud. The English Puritan hopes of a Scotland-like Reformation were waning, and thousands of people, including John Cotton, fled England for American shores.

In 1645–57, Oliver Cromwell ushered in a brief period in which the Puritans gained ascendency in Parliament, and they began to install the Scottish system of Presbyterianism. Thus, some of the most seminal documents of English Protestant Christianity were penned during this span, including the Westminster Confession of Faith of 1646. This one particular statement would serve as a theological starting point for a number of denominations, even for some Baptists and Congregationalists. The Westminster Confession is still considered to be the best summary of Reformed theology in existence.

But with Charles II on the throne, Puritanism was suppressed, and by 1662, complete adherence to the Church of England was enforced. Hundreds of Puritans were forced from their homes, and many were divested of teaching positions, though some remained as a dissenting minority voice. Persecution continued to push Puritanism from the public eye. They quietly faded into history in England, but many of them came to the United States.

On the Mayflower, the Pilgrims had their Geneva Bibles, the primary Bible of sixteenth-century Protestantism. This Bible was carefully translated by scholars who fled from England to Calvin's Geneva, where they could work in the safety of this Protestant region. It was printed in Scotland and distributed both there and in England. This was the first time that a printed Bible was made directly available to the public in those countries. The Bible also came with study notes, verse citations, cross-references, maps, and the like. This Bible, translated in Geneva with Calvin's blessing, is one more way in which Calvinism reached far beyond Switzerland to impact the world.

The Netherlands and the Dutch Reformed Church

Throughout Europe, Calvinist thought was under the thumb of persecution, and the Reformed Christians of the Netherlands were no exception. They too sought freedom from the cruel leadership of the Catholic Church, but unlike in France, they succeeded. Therefore, the story of Calvinism among the Dutch is not defined by tragedy as much as by theological victory.

How had the Reformed church come to prosper here? Early on, martyrs were aplenty in the region, especially among the Augustinian monks who left Catholicism and followed after the teachings of Luther. The city of Antwerp came to house a vibrant Lutheran community, and even though the Catholics continued to persecute Protestants, Calvinists were present by the middle of the sixteenth century. Thanks to the Belgic Confession in 1561, the nobles of the Netherlands started aligning themselves with the Reformed faith to free themselves from Roman Catholicism with its political ties to Spain.

In 1568, William of Orange led a revolt to free the Netherlands from the heavy hand of Spain. William wanted the Spanish Inquisition stopped and all the decrees against heretics withdrawn. He eventually renounced his loyalty to the king of Spain and openly affirmed that he was a Calvinist. When he went into battle he said, "I made an alliance with the mightiest of all Potentates—the God of Hosts, who is able to save us if He choose."[4] In the end, the Spaniards lost the war and their power in the Netherlands along with it. The Netherlands was granted the tolerance William fought for. Even the Anabaptists, considered a scourge elsewhere, found a degree of acceptance in the Netherlands. But with the backing from civil authorities, Reformed ministers had the upper hand in negotiations. And when communities surrendered to the new civil establishment, they handed over their primary places of worship to the Calvinists. Of course, many Catholics saw this as capitulation and so resisted submission to the Protestants. But the Calvinists prevailed.

The Word of God now occupied the most prominent areas in the Netherlands, and the people of the country were encountering the truth where Romish darkness had previously obscured the gospel. This acceptance of Calvinism also led to reforms in government and commerce. Suddenly, the Reformed church had a new problem that many other countries longed to emulate: it had a plethora of pulpits to fill. They knew that training their own ministers in the pattern of Geneva would take time, so they asked that ministers come from other countries to help them.

IACOBUS ARMINIUS.

It was in response to the teaching of Arminius that Calvinists developed the famous TULIP teaching to summarize their doctrine.

For all their successes, the Christian society that the Netherlands longed for was never truly reached, at least not on par with Geneva. The Reformed church was always a minority, with many citizens giving only lip service to the doctrines of the church. Yet the Reformed faith held its own, and as its position stabilized, so did opposition.

A theological controversy arose through the teachings of a Dutch professor named Jacob Arminius (1560–1609). He challenged the prevailing Calvinistic doctrine with its rigid belief that God elects some to eternal life and bypasses others. He believed that Calvinism removed the free will of humanity and, as such, was a stumbling block to many within the Dutch church.

The Dutch church responded with a formal meeting from 1618 to 1619 called the Synod of Dort (referred to in the previous chapter). This council of godly men responded with what we now know as the "five points of Calvinism" and rejected the views of Arminius. This theological victory is perhaps the greatest legacy of the Dutch Calvinists.

Much to the chagrin of the Lutherans, Calvinist thought also penetrated Germany. Even Hungary was reached through the writings of Theodore Beza, who was Calvin's ministerial successor in Geneva. Where Reformed churches didn't thrive, translations of Calvin's works were still disseminated. Unexpectedly, Calvin had a substantial circulation in the Italian language, which undoubtedly annoyed the Vatican.

There was a time when theology was seen as the queen of the sciences. But today, the queen has lost her crown. We forget that it was the doctrines of the sovereignty of God and the depravity of humanity, along with a clear understanding of justification by faith alone, that made the church great. To a large extent, evangelicals are the heirs to a world that was shaped by Christians who followed in the footsteps of Calvin. While we may not share in Calvin's ecclesiology or politics, his doctrines of salvation and his desire for holiness are a welcome tonic for our age.

Just as Calvinism challenged the prevailing distortions of Catholicism in the sixteenth century, in the same way, its teachings can challenge the prevailing distortions in our shallow, consumer-driven evangelicalism of today. Only a robust understanding of the gospel can make the church great again.

How the Reformers Differed

The starting point of theology for Martin Luther was the doctrine of justification by faith. His great motto was "Thou art forgiven!" For

John Calvin, it was "If God be for us, who can be against us?" Luther also believed in God's sovereignty in the affairs of human beings, but his central teaching was the wonder of redemption, whereas Calvin emphasized the certainty of God's purposes.

As for forms of worship, Luther believed that the church should be free to use any modes of worship as long they were not expressly forbidden by Scripture. Thus he retained as much of the form of Catholic worship as possible. In contrast, Calvin and Zwingli worshiped according to the "regulative principle" and permitted only what was expressly commanded in Scripture. Both Swiss Reformers forbade instruments such as the organ because the New Testament makes no reference to worship music among the early Christians.

They also differed over the meaning of the sacraments. Although the Swiss agreed with Luther that the practice of infant baptism should be continued, they differed over its significance. Luther accepted the basic Catholic belief that baptism was the entry point into the Christian life; baptism washes away original sin and makes an infant a child of God

From left to right: William Farel, John Calvin, Theodore Beza, John Knox

because it effects regeneration. Today Lutheran churches continue to believe that "we are born children of fallen humanity; in the waters baptism we are reborn children of God and inheritors of eternal life. As a result, many Lutherans assume that they are Christians bec they were baptized. Of course, the response is that infant faith be nurtured by instruction, such as the catechism and confirmation. But often the basic assumption that one is already a child of God (regenerated) leads the child to believe that there does not have to be a point of conscious conversion; it is enough to give mental assent to the doctrines of the church and reaffirm the meaning of one's infant baptism. The child believes he or she has already been converted.

Zwingli and Calvin retained infant baptism but interpreted it as a sign of the covenant; hence it did not effect any miraculous action on God's part. Although Calvin at one time suggested that baptized infants are already regenerated by God, he dropped that notion because it would mean that elect infants were not born "in Adam" but "in Christ." His more reasonable suggestion was that infant baptism is a sign of "future faith" and a sign that the "seeds of repentance" are in the child and will someday bear fruit. Sometimes it is interpreted as a sign of a covenant that God is making with the parents that their child will someday be regenerated.

Many different arguments have been used to try to connect infant baptism and faith, but in my opinion, each has serious problems. In the midst of this important controversy we must remember that infant baptism is not taught anywhere in the New Testament, nor has an instance of it been recorded in the Scriptures. In the book of Acts, adults were baptized in response to saving faith. And it seems clear that the mode of baptism was immersion.

As for the Lord's Supper, all three of the Reformers were united in their opposition to the Roman Catholic view of transubstantiation, that is, that the elements at the Lord's table are literally the body and blood of Christ and therefore worthy of worship. But when the Reformers set forth their own views, there were differences among them. As we have learned, at his debate with Zwingli, Luther was convinced that the body and blood of Christ are truly present in the elements at the Lord's table. Sometimes this view is called *consubstantiation*, meaning that Christ is present along with the elements; at any rate, it is the true body and blood of Christ that is given and received in the mouths of the participants. As might be expected, the Lutheran church continues to condemn the transubstantiation of Catholicism and also the view that Christ is only spiritually present in the elements (as Calvin believed), or that they are simply symbols of the far distant body and blood of Christ (as Zwingli believed). These differences continue between the Lutheran and Reformed churches today.

Regarding the state, Luther allowed it a great deal of authority, stressing the need for obedience to the political powers. Calvin and Zwingli were less inclined. Also—and this is important for Luther—Luther was adamant that no person should ever fight under the banner of the cross; that is, Protestants should not go to war against the Catholics, nor should the Catholics have gone to war against the Turks under the banner of Christianity. This explains why, when Zwingli died as a chaplain in a Protestant army, Luther believed that his death was the judgment of God for using the sword to defend Christ's church. However, Luther did believe that if the state asked a Christian to fight, he should do so with implicit obedience.

Despite these differences, that which united them was greater than that which divided them. It's a reminder that we don't have to agree on various issues in order to be used by God. Standing in the nonnegotiable center, however, are the cries of the Reformation: *sola Scriptura; sola gratia; sola fide; solus Christus; and soli Deo gloria* (Scripture alone, grace alone, faith alone, Christ alone, to the glory of God alone).

On this we stake our lives and our eternity.

17

Is the Reformation Over?

Brothers and sisters, Luther's protest is over. Is yours?"
Those are the words of the late Episcopal bishop Tony Palmer, who spoke to a cheering crowd of followers of charismatic teacher Kenneth Copeland. Through Palmer's efforts, high-profile Protestant ministers met with Pope Francis in 2014. Clearly, this pope gladly embraces Protestants and desires to work with them to bring about unity and spread Christianity to the world. After Jorge Bergoglio became Pope Francis in 2012, evangelist Luis Palau reported that he had worked with the new pope back in Argentina. So, we are told, the stage is set for continuing unity between the two groups.

With the new openness between evangelicals and Catholics, we shouldn't be surprised that some evangelicals are turning to the Catholic Church both for instruction on practices, such as contemplative prayer, and for joint ventures in worship and mission. Evangelical pastors and institutions are forging bonds with Catholics to demonstrate the unity of the church and to explore common ground between them. This sounds like such a wonderful idea that many evangelicals wonder why this isn't done more often in our churches, Bible colleges, and seminaries. Furthermore, since the accord on the *Doctrine of Justification by Faith* was signed between Catholics and Protestants in Augsburg, Germany, on October 31, 1999 (which some believe reached agreement on justification), praying together and exploring mission together seemed like the next step. After all, Jesus said unity was to be a powerful sign of His presence among His people.

In 2005, the well-respected historian Mark A. Noll along with Carolyn Nystrom wrote a book titled *Is the Reformation Over?*[1] Their answer, in short, is *yes*—but not quite. They acknowledge that differences between Catholicism and Protestantism still remain, but as for the Reformation in the sixteenth century, *that* reformation, they say, is over. The lines between Catholicism and evangelicalism are no longer distinct. We have entered a new era of unity, compromise, and shared mission.

The late Charles Colson of Prison Fellowship gave momentum to this unity when he, along with Richard Neuhaus, published their "Evangelicals and Catholics Together" document in 1994.[2] What at one time seemed to be unthinkable was now being thought about by many evangelicals who discovered that there were Catholics who shared a love for Christ and were concerned about the moral and spiritual decline of the West.

Mark Noll's book is replete with accounts of meetings between Catholics and evangelicals and details on how close they seem to come in agreement. The Second Vatican Council (1962–65), which had a charitable view of Protestants, calling them "separated brethren," opened the door for collaboration and dialogue. Some Catholic churches now have Bible studies, and there even seems to be a growing evangelical understanding of the gospel in many parishes.

Noll summarizes the various dialogues between Catholics, Lutherans, and evangelicals by saying, "Thirty-five years of ecumenical discussion revealed a surprising range of agreements between Protestants and

Catholics."[3] As a result of these carefully worded statements on which both sides could agree, some measure of unity has been achieved. Noll admits that on the matter of salvation there was continuing disagreement as evangelicals emphasize salvation as a one-time event (conversion), while Catholics stress that it is a lifelong process. And yet, despite these differences, Protestants and Catholics agree on this statement: "We recognize that our justification is a totally gratuitous work accomplished by God in Christ. We confess that the acceptance in faith of justification is itself a gift of grace. . . . To rely for salvation on anything other than faith would be to diminish the fullness accomplished and offered in Jesus Christ."[4]

The concord between Lutherans and Catholics of 1999 asserted that "Justification is the forgiveness of sins. . . . It is acceptance into communion with God. . . . It occurs in the reception of the Holy Spirit in baptism and incorporation into the one body. All this is from God alone, for Christ's sake, by grace, though faith, in 'the gospel of God's Son.'"[5]

If you carefully reread the above statement, you'll realize that it's actually fully consistent with Catholic theology. The Catholic Church has always taught that Christ died for our sins; it has always believed that we are forgiven by our faith and the grace given to the penitent in *cooperation with and through the sacraments beginning with baptism.* Catholicism has always presented the doctrine of justification as one of divine pardon and the renewal of the inner person, but additional requirements have been added. What Catholicism has always denied is that salvation is a free gift of imputed righteousness given in response to saving faith alone.

The Gospel Compromised

Where does all this leave us? Alas, many evangelicals, myself included, grieve at the thought that the precious gospel of our Lord Jesus Christ is being severely compromised for the sake of ecumenism. We welcome the good will that has developed between evangelicals and Catholics and are glad that we can cooperate on such issues as opposition to same-sex marriage and abortion, along with fighting for freedom of religion and other such matters. But when it comes to the central issue of the gospel, the gap between us is just as wide as ever. Indeed, although there might appear to be some similarities between Catholics and Protestants on this issue, the differences remain. On the most critical issue, namely the salvation of the human soul, Luther's Reformation is far from over.

Of course, individuals within the Catholic Church are being converted today as the Scriptures are being studied. There are some priests in the West who are quite evangelical in their thinking. (In Chicago, Cardinal Bernardin, who died many years ago, was open to the evangelical faith.) But the Catholic Church has not changed its official position (nor did Bernardin) that human merit cooperates in the process of salvation. As a graduate of Loyola University in Chicago, I've had years of firsthand confirmation that no matter how many changes the Catholic Church makes, it *will* not—indeed *cannot*—endorse an evangelical view of salvation.

First, there can be no unity on the gospel of salvation without discussing indulgences, prayers to Mary, purgatory, and the like. The fact that after years of dialogue between the two groups, Catholics and evangelicals were able to create a statement that brings them to "close agreement" on the many issues that divide them hardly closes the gap between the two belief systems, and it by no means signals the end of the Reformation.

John Calvin warned against this kind of verbal agreement on justification, as if a statement about salvation could transcend the differences between the two groups. Even in his day attempts were made to unify the church. Catholic authorities presented a document that affirmed justification by faith, but it was shrouded within a Catholic context.

But for Calvin, a slogan could not stand alone. The truths of the gospel are presented within a larger context and depend on one another. All the individual statements of doctrine must cohere within a doctrinal framework. In other words, it doesn't do any good to say that Catholics adhere to justification by faith if they continue practicing indulgences and penance, praying to Mary and the saints, venerating relics, giving last rites to the dying, performing masses for the dead, and, in short, teaching that saving grace is given through the sacraments. Despite verbal agreement, said Calvin, the Catholic Church robs God of His glory by such practices along with the vigils, the use of rosaries, and the worship of the elements in the mass.

Furthermore, while the doctrine of justification is central for Protestants (the doctrine on which the church stands or falls), it is only on the periphery for Catholics. "American Cardinal Avery Dulles admits, 'Justification is rarely discussed at length except in polemics against, or dialogue with, Protestants.' Lutheran scholar James Preuss once stated the problem even more baldly, 'The doctrine [of justification] is at best at the fringe of their *corpus doctrinae*, like a fingernail, or like the planet Pluto at the edge of our solar system.'"[6] To reach verbal agreement on justification changes nothing if these other doctrines are not addressed.

Scholars sitting in a room stretching their own convictions to make them more palatable to one another hardly constitute significant agreement. For centuries, the Catholic Church has held to dogmas that contradict (and even condemn) the doctrine of justification by faith alone (such as those of the Council of Trent). They've never been denied and are still actively taught despite the years of dialogue.

Today it's fashionable to say that the Apostles' Creed is a sufficient basis for unity. But the Apostles' Creed doesn't contain a clear exposition of the gospel, nor does it explain how the gospel is to be received. Although we are thankful for the recitation of the basic doctrines of the Christian faith listed in the creed, it is silent about how salvation is received. This explains why it can be adopted by both Catholics and evangelicals without resolving the differences between the two.

The prayer of Jesus in John 17 is often quoted by those who desire to bring the two groups together because, they say, Jesus prayed that all of His children would be "one." But in context, Jesus is referring to all those who are truly His, not those who just claim His name. There is no doubt that His prayer was answered on the day of Pentecost and is being answered today by the baptism of the Spirit, which is given to all believers (1 Cor. 12:13). It is further answered as believers meet together in the name of Christ and demonstrate their love for one another and the world. Certainly we should strive toward unity among believers, but the prayer isn't fulfilled through unity that includes those who clearly adhere to a false gospel.

Contemporary Teachings

We are often told that contemporary Catholicism is quite different from that in decades or centuries gone by. Certainly, Catholicism in the United States has a more open attitude toward evangelicals than that which exists in predominantly Catholic countries in other parts of the world. But that being said, let us take a moment to review a few teachings of the 1994 *Catechism of the Catholic Church* to see what, if anything, has changed. By doing so, we'll discover that the church still holds to the traditions it has always held about Mary, her perpetual virginity, her immaculate conception (which denies the biblical truth that all have sinned), the assumption of her body and soul into heaven (promulgated by Pope Pius XII in 1950), the queenship of heaven, and—most serious of all—the "infallible" teaching that she is the mediatrix of all grace, thus sharing with the Lord Jesus Christ in providing salvation for mankind. The catechism says, "By her intercession she continues to bring us the gifts of eternal salvation. . . . Therefore the Blessed Virgin is invoked in the Church under the titles of Advocate, Helper, Benefactress, and Mediatrix." It is to her "protection that the faithful fly in all their dangers and needs."[7]

This is consistent with a handbook for priests published in 1955 that says, "Mary, by her spiritual entering into the sacrifice of her Divine Son for men, made atonement for the sins of men, and . . . merited the application of the redemptive grace of Christ. In this manner she co-operates in the subjective redemption of mankind."[8] A Catholic devotional book says, "Mary is called . . . the gate of heaven, because no one can enter that blessed kingdom without passing through her."[9]

In European churches, where we often find a purer form of Catholicism, I have seen paintings of Jesus lifting the crown from His head and putting it on Mary, the "Queen of Heaven." Space forbids me to go into detail about the role of Mary in the Catholic Church, but I must humbly affirm that the adoration given to her is blasphemous. In a discussion with a Catholic theologian, I made the remark that I didn't believe Mary has heard a single prayer offered to her, to which he remarked, "Mary has heard all the prayers to her that God wants her to hear." I agreed with him, but pointed out that there is no scriptural evidence that God wants her to hear any prayers. I sincerely hope that God mercifully shields her from any awareness of the continuous daily adoration given to her by multiplied millions on Earth. Although the Catholic Church teaches that Mary is to be adored but not worshiped, the distinction is lost among the millions who bow before her, pray to her, and give her their affections.

Transubstantiation

The 1994 *Catechism of the Catholic Church* approvingly quotes the Council of Trent in its defense of transubstantiation, that is, that the consecrated bread and wine become the *actual* body and blood of Christ in every mass.[10] The Eucharist is the "source and summit of the Christian life" and the "cause of that communion in the divine life."[11] More than this, "The sacrifice of Christ and the sacrifice of the Eucharist are one single sacrifice. . . . 'The same Christ who offered himself once in a bloody manner on the altar of the cross is contained and offered in an unbloody manner.'"[12] Catholics are taught to worship the consecrated wafer when displayed in a monstrance (a tabernacle). Indeed, parishioners are instructed to give these consecrated elements the highest form of worship—the same degree reserved for the Holy Trinity. Historically (and to this present day) the Catholic Church has taught that salvation comes *only* through the grace given in the sacraments, which, they say, unite the participant to Christ.

Several Catholics have told me that their priest has said that if they skip mass (unless they are unable to attend because of illness or an emergency), they have committed a mortal sin—a sin that will condemn them to hell. No wonder so many Catholics don't know whether God is pleased or angry with them. It's so difficult to keep track of all the pluses and minuses of one's ever-vacillating relationship with Him.

Indulgences

What about the doctrine of indulgences that sparked the Reformation? As already quoted in the third chapter of this book, the recent *Catechism of the Catholic Church* (published 1994) defines an indulgence as "a remission before God of the temporal punishment due to sins whose guilt has already been forgiven. . . . An indulgence is partial or plenary according as it removes either part or all of the temporal punishment due to sin. Indulgences may be applied to the living or the dead."[13] What follows that statement is a discussion of the distinction between mortal sins (which, if not addressed, lead to eternal punishment) and venial sins (which, if not purified here on earth, lead to purgatory). Yes, the *Catechism* teaches that these indulgences are not only for the living but can also be applied to the dead.

And if you still think that this doctrine was taught only in medieval times, we were recently reminded that the official teaching of the church hasn't changed since then. As I mentioned back in chapter 3, when Pope Francis visited Brazil for World Youth Day in 2013, the Vatican offered a plenary (complete) indulgence to those who couldn't attend the event but followed on Twitter or by other means. The difference between today and days gone by is that indulgences are no longer sold as such; they are obtained by following prescribed rituals and showing proper devotion to God as requested by the pope. I realize that official Catholic theology says that indulgences do not remit eternal penalties (which can be forgiven only by God), but indulgences do remit temporal penalties, including purgatory.

I have visited Rome several times, and each time I notice that information about obtaining indulgences can be found at the airport. Just as in Luther's day, people make spiritual pilgrimages to Rome to procure indulgences, visit relics, and seek divine favor by burning candles or saying special prayers. Catholics who make the rounds in Rome are hoping that in the end "it all adds up" toward a better final score.

Millions of Catholics will attend church this coming Sunday, confessing their sins just as Luther did in the monastery, but they will have no assurance that they have been permanently received by God. They expect that their confession will at best cover past sins, so that if they died right after the mass they might have a good chance of making it to heaven. Many will fear that if they died on a Wednesday, they would have no opportunity to confess more recent sins and get "caught up to date with God."

Unfortunately these millions almost certainly will not be told the gospel; namely, "But when Christ had offered for all time a single sacrifice for sins, he sat down on the right hand of God. . . . For by a single offering he has perfected for all time those who are being sanctified" (see Heb. 10:12–14). If they turned away from their own attempts at righteousness and believed this good news for themselves, they would have the assurance of God's promises and the inner witness of the Holy Spirit (Rom. 8:16). The New Testament teaches that Christ isn't simply *necessary* for our salvation; *He is all we need for our salvation.*

Superstitions

In St. Peter's Basilica, long lines of people stand before a statue of the apostle to touch (or kiss) his toe. I asked our tour guide about this, and she said, "We have this tradition that if you touch Peter's toe and die you go directly to heaven and bypass purgatory." Of course, these superstitions are not a part of Catholic theology. But why would Rome—in the very Vatican no less!—foster and encourage these kinds of superstitions that mislead millions? Why aren't the priests, in Rome or the West, condemning these kinds of abuses? What difference does an accord on justification with Protestants make as long as crowds continue to line up in the Vatican to touch the toe of Peter in order to receive special blessings, perhaps even the promise of eternal life?

Throughout the cities of the world, crowds line up when a relic is on display. And if a statue begins to "weep," people throng to get a glimpse of it. In a rural New Mexico town in 1978, Mario Rubio was rolling a burrito and noticed that the skillet burns on a tortilla looked like the face of Jesus. Soon eight thousand pilgrims came to his family's small stucco house to view this icon and receive a blessing. Here in Chicago, water leaking through cracks in a viaduct appeared to form the face of Mary. Cars of people wanting to get a glimpse lined up for blocks. Where is the public condemnation by priests, archbishops, and cardinals? Why aren't they denouncing these kinds of responses? People should be warned that these superstitions distract them from the Scriptures and give them false hope.

Bringing Protestants and Catholics together through a nuanced verbal agreement does not nullify the superstitions, abuses, and official teaching of the church, nor does it result in a powerful witness of a unified church.

Sainthood

And what about sainthood? The New Testament repeatedly refers to all Christians as saints (Eph. 1:1; Phil. 1:1). However, on April 27, 2014, two popes were canonized because they qualified for sainthood by performing at least two miracles after they died. Clearly, the Catholic Church has a different understanding of justification and a different understanding of glorification. This deserves much more discussion than I can give it here.

Sometimes I hear Protestants say that since the Catholic Church worships the true God, we should overlook its layers of tradition and superstitions. But during the time Jesus walked on earth, the Pharisees also worshiped the true God of Abraham, Isaac, and Jacob, yet He said of them, "In vain do they worship me, teaching as doctrines the commandments of men" (Mark 7:7). Yes, the traditions of men negated their worship of God and turned it into vanity.

The Catholic Church has been (and still is) strongly opposed to the conviction that we are saved by faith alone because of grace alone through Christ alone. My point is that either salvation is a free gift of God's righteousness imparted in response to faith, or salvation necessitates our cooperation. Either the righteousness we receive is wholly a gift of God given directly in response to saving faith or it's mediated through baptism, mass, last rites, or other sacraments and combined with good deeds. These positions cannot be reconciled.

Is the Reformation over? Certainly the complexity of the Reformation of the sixteenth century with all of its conflicts that permanently changed the map of Europe—*that* Reformation is over. But the doctrines that Luther and Calvin stood against—that aspect of the Reformation is not over. It is as relevant as a discussion I had with a priest who said that the suffering of drug addicts contributes to their own salvation because they are entering into the sufferings of Christ—even if their ordeal is self-inflicted. It is as relevant as the devout Catholic who told me that he expected to go to heaven because he was wearing a "scapular" (an object or pendant worn around the neck that will serve as last rites should he die unexpectedly). It is as relevant as my visit to the shrine of Guadalupe, where I saw hundreds of people, among them young mothers with babies in their arms, inching along on their bleeding knees hoping to get a blessing from the Virgin Mary. It is as relevant as a lapsed Catholic who told me that he didn't know where he stood with God at any given moment, that he felt somewhat better after the mass but was plunged into despair after his next sin: uncertainty, failure, and more uncertainty.

As for Pope Francis, he wrote only one book before he was elevated to the papacy, titled *The History of the Jesuits*.[14] In it he says that the Reformation is the root of all the evils in the Western world. Yet, today he is courting evangelicals so that they might become "evangelical Catholics." History shows that they will be added to the church but not permitted to reform it.

Our Modern Dilemma

Why should evangelicals and Catholics not pray in one another's churches and explore mission together? Simply put, such visible signs of unity give the wrong impressions. Perceptions are incredibly important. When Paul went to Galatia, he stood up to Peter and sharply rebuked him. "I opposed him to his face, because he stood condemned" (Gal. 2:11). Why? Was he presenting a false gospel? No, Peter was straight on the gospel and had not compromised his message. But he was rebuked for failure to eat with gentiles when the Judaizers arrived. In other words, he gave the *impression* that he agreed with the Judaizers, who taught that salvation was through Christ in conjunction with the keeping of the law. Just a false impression was enough for Paul to react.

Just a false impression that the evangelical doctrine of salvation and that of the Roman Catholic Church are one and the same is enough to confuse and mislead the faithful. About 20 percent of the members of the Moody Church, where I've been the pastor for thirty-five years, were raised in the Catholic Church. They are dismayed when they are told that the two groups are essentially one, or that there can be some kind of shared gospel unity. They know firsthand that the gospel they grew up with was not a free gift given to repentant sinners; it was a matter of sacraments, candles, prayers, and indulgences along with the help of Mary—and yes, of course, with the help of Jesus's sacrifice too! But all of these added together couldn't give them assurance that they had ever done enough for God.

In summary, those who teach that the Reformation is over disregard the official teachings of the Catholic Church and pin their hopes on scholars sitting in a room forging an agreement. Even if such unity is achieved, it has little effect on the actual teachings that are still promulgated in most Catholic churches. The fact that there are some born-again believers in the Catholic Church is good news, but it doesn't affect the character of the church as a whole.

No doubt there are many unnecessary divisions within the church today, but some are necessary when the doctrine of salvation is at issue. Yes, we must strive toward unity, but unity should not cause us to compromise the central doctrine of the Scriptures. As the old saying goes, "It is more important to be divided by truth than it is to be united by error."

To Rescue the Gospel

Martin Luther had to rescue the gospel from the distortions of Catholicism; in some sense, our task is more difficult than his. We must rescue the gospel from Catholicism along with a host of other movements, such as fraudulent, so-called evangelicals whose entire television (or internet) programs are dedicated to "health and wealth" theology with special "breakthroughs" promised to those who send them money. We have to rescue it from theological liberals who deny the supernatural character of the Christian faith. We have to rescue it from false religions that compete for the allegiance of men and women.

We must rescue it from the cults who come to our doorsteps; we must rescue it from all who think that it is up to them to contribute to their salvation and that they must make themselves worthy to receive it. We must remind the world that the gospel of the New Testament is for the spiritually needy who have nothing to offer God; they come not to give but to receive; they come not just to be helped but to be rescued. Their contribution to salvation is their sin; God's grace supplies everything else.

The apostle Paul knew that every era had to be vigilant.

> Pay careful attention to yourselves and to all the flock, in which the Holy Spirit has made you overseers, to care for the church of God, which he obtained with his own blood. I know that after my departure fierce wolves will come in among you, not sparing the flock; and from among your own selves will arise men speaking twisted things, to draw away the disciples after them. Therefore be alert. . . . And now I commend you to God and to the word of his grace, which is able to build you up and to give you the inheritance among all those who are sanctified. (Acts 20:28–32)

This is our task in every age.

Notes

Introduction: Join Me on a Journey

1. Quoted in Alister McGrath, *Christian Theology: An Introduction*, 5th ed. (Malden, MA: Wiley-Blackwell, 2011), 108.

Chapter 1 Power, Scandals, and Corruption

1. Justo L. González, *The Story of Christianity* (Peabody, MA: Prince, 2001), 2:6.

2. Andrea Di Strumi, "Pataria," in *Medieval Italy: Texts in Translation*, ed. Katherine L. Jansen, Joanna Drell, and Frances Andrews, trans. William North (Philadelphia: University of Pennsylvania Press, 2009), 339.

3. John Foxe, *Foxe's Book of Martyrs* (Uhrichsville, OH: Barbour, 2001), 37.

Chapter 2 A Morning Star and a Goose and Swan

1. Bruce L. Shelley, *Church History in Plain Language* (Waco: Word, 1982), 250.

2. Shelley, *Church History*, 250.

3. http://legacy.fordham.edu/halsall/mod/14 15janhus.asp/.

4. Matthew Spinka, *John Hus and the Council of Constance* (New York: Columbia University Press, 1965), 230.

5. Spinka, *John Hus*, 233.

6. Spinka, *John Hus*, 233.

7. Martin Luther, *Commentary on the Alleged Imperial Edict Promulgated in the Year 1531*, quoted in Heiko A. Oberman, *Luther: Man between God and the Devil*, trans. Eileen Walliser-Schwarzbart (New York: Image, 1982), 55.

Chapter 3 The Wittenberg Door

1. Quoted in William Roscoe Estep, *Renaissance and Reformation* (Grand Rapids: Eerdmans, 1986), 107.

2. Roland H. Bainton, *Here I Stand: A Life of Martin Luther* (New York: Mentor, 1950), 56.

3. Bainton, *Here I Stand*, 57.

4. *The Catechism of the Catholic Church* (New York: Doubleday, 1995), 411.

5. http://www.news.va/en/news/papal-indul gences-for-world-youth-day.

6. Bainton, *Here I Stand*, 59.

7. Bainton, *Here I Stand*, 60.

8. John D. Woodbridge and Frank A. James III, *Church History* (Grand Rapids: Zondervan, 2013), 2:107.

9. Timothy F. Lull, ed., *Martin Luther's Basic Theological Writings* (Minneapolis: Fortress, 1989), 21–28.

10. Bainton, *Here I Stand*, 65.

11. Bainton, *Here I Stand*, 65.

Chapter 4 Who Was Martin Luther?

1. Roland H. Bainton, *Here I Stand: A Life of Martin Luther* (New York: Mentor, 1950), 26.

2. Bainton, *Here I Stand*, 26.
3. Bainton, *Here I Stand*, 28.
4. Bainton, *Here I Stand*, 30.
5. Bainton, *Here I Stand*, 31.
6. Bainton, *Here I Stand*, 34.
7. Bainton, *Here I Stand*, 37.
8. Heiko A. Oberman, *Luther: Man between God and the Devil*, trans. Eileen Walliser-Schwarzbart (New York: Image, 1982), 149.
9. Oberman, *Luther*, 149.

Chapter 5 The Great Discovery

1. Roland H. Bainton, *Here I Stand: A Life of Martin Luther* (New York: Mentor, 1950), 41.
2. Bainton, *Here I Stand*, 41.
3. Bainton, *Here I Stand*, 42.
4. Bainton, *Here I Stand*, 45.
5. Bainton, *Here I Stand*, 49.
6. See Luther's letter to George Spenlein, April 8, 1516, in *Luther: Letters of Spiritual Counsel*, ed. and trans. Theodore G. Tappert, Library of Christian Classics (Philadelphia: Westminster, 1960), 110.
7. James Kittleson, *Luther the Reformer* (Minneapolis: Fortress, 2003), 107.
8. Bainton, *Here I Stand*, 66.
9. Kittleson, *Luther the Reformer*, 112.
10. Kittleson, *Luther the Reformer*, 112.
11. Kittleson, *Luther the Reformer*, 112.
12. Bainton, *Here I Stand*, 71.
13. Bainton, *Here I Stand*, 79.
14. Kittleson, *Luther the Reformer*, 138.
15. Bainton, *Here I Stand*, 90.
16. Bainton, *Here I Stand*, 92.

Chapter 6 The Dominoes Begin to Fall

1. Philip Schaff, *History of the Christian Church* (1910; repr., Grand Rapids: Eerdmans, 1980), 7:206–7.
2. Heiko A. Oberman, *Luther: Man between God and the Devil*, trans. Eileen Walliser-Schwarzbart (New York: Image, 1982), 43.
3. Roland H. Bainton, *Here I Stand: A Life of Martin Luther* (New York: Mentor, 1950), 119.
4. Quoted in R. Paul Stevens, *The Other Six Days: Vocation, Work, and Ministry in Biblical Perspective* (Grand Rapids: Eerdmans, 2000), 77.

5. *Luther: Selected Political Writings*, ed. J. M. Porter (Philadelphia: Fortress, 1971), 44.
6. *Luther: Selected Political Writings*, 46.
7. Schaff, *History of the Christian Church*, 7:209–10.
8. Schaff, *History of the Christian Church*, 7:14.
9. Reinhold Seeberg, *Textbook of the History of Christian Doctrines*, trans. Charles E. Hay (Grand Rapids: Baker, 1964), 1:68.
10. Alphonse de Liguori, *The Dignity and Duties of the Priest* (Milwaukee: Our Blessed Lady of Victory Mission, 1927), 1.1.3.
11. Philip Schaff, *The Creeds of Christendom* (Grand Rapids: Baker, 1983), 2:131.
12. Bainton, *Here I Stand*, 107.
13. Bainton, *Here I Stand*, 109.
14. Quoted in James Kittleson, *Luther the Reformer* (Minneapolis: Fortress, 2003), 153.
15. Schaff, *History of the Christian Church*, 7:16.

Chapter 7 The Wild Boar in the Vineyard of the Lord

1. Roland H. Bainton, *Here I Stand: A Life of Martin Luther* (New York: Mentor, 1950), 114.
2. Bainton, *Here I Stand*, 141.
3. Bainton, *Here I Stand*, 115.
4. Bainton, *Here I Stand*, 115.
5. Bainton, *Here I Stand*, 116.
6. Bainton, *Here I Stand*, 126.
7. Martin Luther, *The Freedom of a Christian*, in *Martin Luther's Basic Theological Writings*, ed. Timothy E. Lull (Minneapolis: Fortress, 1989), 593.
8. Luther, *Freedom of a Christian*, 588.
9. Luther, *Freedom of a Christian*, 596.
10. Luther, *Freedom of a Christian*, 623.
11. Luther, *Freedom of a Christian*, 619.
12. Luther, *Freedom of a Christian*, 619.
13. Bainton, *Here I Stand*, 124.
14. Bainton, *Here I Stand*, 127–28.
15. Bainton, *Here I Stand*, 128–29 (emphasis mine).
16. Henry Clay Vedder, *The Reformation in Germany* (London: Macmillan, 1914), 140.
17. Hans Hillerbrand, ed., *The Reformation: A Narrative History Related by Contemporary Observers and Participants* (Grand Rapids: Baker, 1991), 85.

18. Hillerbrand, *Reformation*, 86.

Chapter 8 Here I Stand

1. Roland H. Bainton, *Here I Stand: A Life of Martin Luther* (New York: Mentor, 1950), 137.

2. Bainton, *Here I Stand*, 139.

3. Bainton, *Here I Stand*, 139.

4. David Otis Fuller, *A Treasury of Evangelical Writings* (Grand Rapids: Kregel, 1974), 119.

5. Bainton, *Here I Stand*, 144.

6. Bainton, *Here I Stand*, 144.

7. Bainton, *Here I Stand*, 145.

8. Bainton, *Here I Stand*, 147.

9. Bainton, *Here I Stand*, 150.

10. Bainton, *Here I Stand*, 151.

11. Heiko A. Oberman, *Luther: Man between God and the Devil*, trans. Eileen Walliser-Schwarzbart (New York: Image, 1982), 104.

12. Oberman, *Luther*, 105.

13. Oberman, *Luther*, 105–6.

14. Oberman, *Luther*, 177.

15. Oberman, *Luther*, 179.

16. Bainton, *Here I Stand*, 284.

17. Bainton, *Here I Stand*, 159–60.

18. Bainton, *Here I Stand*, 207.

19. Martin Luther, *Against the Heavenly Prophets*, in *Luther's Works*, vol. 40, *Church and Ministry II*, ed. Helmut H. Lehman (Philadelphia: Fortress, 1958), 222.

Chapter 9 We Are Protestants Now

1. Roland Bainton, *The Reformation of the Sixteenth Century* (Boston: Beacon, 1952), 149.

2. John D. Woodbridge and Frank A. James III, *Church History*, vol. 2, *From Pre-Reformation to the Present Day* (Grand Rapids: Zondervan, 2013), 137.

3. http://en.wikisource.org/wiki/Augsburg_Confession.

4. Woodbridge and James, *Church History*, 2:138.

5. Woodbridge and James, *Church History*, 2:138.

6. Bainton, *Reformation of the Sixteenth Century*, 155.

7. Martin Rinkart, "Now Thank We All Our God," trans. Catherine Winkworth, in *The English Hymnal with Tunes* (London: Oxford University Press, 1933), no. 533.

Chapter 10 Disputes, Disunity, and Destiny

1. Martin Luther, *An Admonition to Peace*, quoted in *Luther: Selected Political Writings*, ed. J. M. Porter (Philadelphia: Fortress, 1974), 72.

2. Luther, *Admonition*, 75.

3. Martin Luther, *Against the Robbing and Murdering Hordes of Peasants*, quoted in *Luther: Selected Political Writings*, 86 (italics mine).

4. Luther, *Against the Robbing and Murdering Hordes*, 87.

5. Martin Luther, *An Open Letter on the Harsh Book against the Peasants*, quoted in *Luther: Selected Political Writings*, 90.

6. Luther, *An Open Letter on the Harsh Book*, 92.

7. Luther, *An Open Letter on the Harsh Book*, 93.

8. Luther, *An Open Letter on the Harsh Book*, 93.

9. Martin Luther, *Whether Soldiers, Too, Can Be Saved*, quoted in *Luther: Selected Political Writings*, 104.

10. Barmen Confession; quoted in Peter Matheson, ed., *The Third Reich and the Christian Churches* (Grand Rapids: Eerdmans, 1981), 46.

11. This section contains material that has been summarized from *The Doctrines That Divide: A Fresh Look at the Historic Doctrines That Separate Christians*, 2nd ed. (Grand Rapids: Kregel, 1998). Thanks to Kregel Publications for permission for its use.

12. Martin Luther, *The Bondage of the Will*, trans. Henry Cole (Grand Rapids: Baker, 1976), 36.

13. See, for instance, Erasmus Middleton, "Life of Martin Luther, the Great Reformer," in Martin Luther, *A Commentary on St. Paul's Epistle to the Galatians* (London: James Cundee, 1807), viii, xli.

14. Quoted in E. Gordon Rupp, introduction to *Luther and Erasmus: Free Will and Salvation*, ed. E. Gordon Rupp, Library of Christian Classics (Philadelphia: Westminster, 1969), 2.

15. Luther, *Bondage*, 69.

16. Luther, *Bondage*, 69–70.

17. Luther, *Bondage*, 159.

18. Luther, *Bondage*, 183.

19. Luther, *Bondage*, 70.

20. Luther, *Bondage*, 73.

21. For those who are interested in reading more about the free will versus predestination debate, I devoted four chapters to this discussion in my book *The Doctrines That Divide*.

22. William L. Shirer, *The Rise and Fall of the Third Reich: A History of Nazi Germany* (New York: Simon & Schuster, 1959), 91.

23. Martin Luther, *On the Jews and Their Lies*, in *Luther's Works*, vol. 47, ed. Martin Bertram (Philadelphia: Fortress, 1971), 268–72.

24. Luther, *On the Jews*, 268–70.

25. Martin Luther, *The Christian in Society II*, in *Luther's Works*, vol. 45, ed. Helmut T. Lehmann and James Atkinson (Philadelphia: Fortress, 1962), 229.

Chapter 11 Luther and the Bible

1. James Kittleson, *Luther the Reformer* (Minneapolis: Fortress, 2003), 113.

2. Heiko Oberman, *Luther: Man between God and the Devil*, trans. Eileen Walliser-Schwarzbart (New York: Image, 1982), 169.

3. Philip Schaff, *History of the Christian Church* (1910; repr., Grand Rapids: Eerdmans, 1980), 7:35.

4. Quoted in Schaff, *History of the Christian Church*, 7:35.

5. http://www.vatican.va/archive/hist_coun cils/ii_vatican_council/documents/vat-ii_const _19651118_dei-verbum_en.html.

6. John Warwick Montgomery, "Lessons from Luther on the Inerrancy of Holy Writ," *Westminster Theological Journal* 36 (1974): 286.

7. Montgomery, "Lessons from Luther," 279–80.

8. Martin Luther, *Table Talk*, in *Luther's Works*, vol. 54, ed. Theodore G. Tappert and Helmut T. Lehmann (Philadelphia: Fortress, 1967), 3.

9. Luther, *Table Talk*, 3.

10. Kittleson, *Luther the Reformer*, 190.

11. Oberman, *Luther*, 172–73.

12. Oberman, *Luther*, 172–73.

13. Oberman, *Luther*, 172–73.

14. Ruth H. Sanders, *German: Biography of a Language* (Oxford: Oxford University Press, 2010), 122.

15. http://www.economist.com/node/167 40435.

16. Eric Solsten, *Germany: A Country Study* (Washington, DC: Library of Congress, 1999), 20.

Chapter 12 Luther, Katie, Children, and Death

1. Roland H. Bainton, *Here I Stand: A Life of Martin Luther* (New York: Mentor, 1950), 223.

2. Bainton, *Here I Stand*, 226.

3. Philip Schaff, *History of the Christian Church* (1910; repr., Grand Rapids: Eerdmans, 1980), 7:461.

4. Bainton, *Here I Stand*, 225.

5. Bainton, *Here I Stand*, 230–31.

6. Schaff, *History of the Christian Church*, 7:462.

7. Schaff, *History of the Christian Church*, 7:462.

8. Bainton, *Here I Stand*, 236–37.

9. Schaff, *History of the Christian Church*, 7:463.

10. Bainton, *Here I Stand*, 237.

11. Schaff, *History of the Christian Church*, 7:465.

12. Schaff, *History of the Christian Church*, 7:465.

13. John D. Woodbridge and Frank A. James III, *Church History*, vol. 2, *From Pre-Reformation to the Present Day* (Grand Rapids: Zondervan, 2013), 141.

14. Schaff, *History of the Christian Church*, 7:299.

15. Martin Luther, sermon on Matt. 11:25–30, February 15, 1546, Eisleben, Germany, in *Luther's Works*, vol. 51, *Sermons I*, ed. John W. Doberstein and Helmut T. Lehmann (Philadelphia: Fortress, 1959), 383.

Chapter 13 Zwingli: Reforming Zurich

1. Timothy George, *Theology of the Reformers* (Nashville: Broadman, 1998), 114.

2. Roland H. Bainton, *The Reformation of the Sixteenth Century* (Boston: Beacon, 1952), 86.

3. Bainton, *Reformation*, 89.

4. Bainton, *Reformation*, 90.

5. This section contains material that has been summarized from *The Doctrines That Divide: A Fresh Look at the Historic Doctrines*

That Separate Christians, 2nd ed. (Grand Rapids: Kregel, 1998). Thanks to Kregel Publications for permission for its use.

6. Donald J. Ziegler, ed., *Great Debates of the Reformation* (New York: Random House, 1969), 71–107.

7. Bainton, *Reformation*, 93.

Chapter 14 The Anabaptists: Promise and Persecution

1. William R. Estep, *The Anabaptist Story* (Grand Rapids: Eerdmans, 1963), 13–14.

2. Estep, *Anabaptist Story*, 11.

3. Roland H. Bainton, *The Reformation of the Sixteenth Century* (Boston: Beacon, 1952), 101–2.

4. Bainton, *Reformation*, 97.

5. Bainton, *Reformation*, 97.

6. Hans Hillerbrand, ed., *The Reformation: A Narrative History Related by Contemporary Observers and Participants* (Grand Rapids: Baker, 1972), 233.

7. Bainton, *Reformation*, 105.

8. Bainton, *Reformation*, 102.

Chapter 15 Calvin: Reforming Geneva

1. Timothy George, *Theology of the Reformers* (Nashville: Broadman, 1988), 180.

2. John Calvin, *Institutes of the Christian Religion* 3.21.1–2, trans. Robert Van Voorst in *Readings in Christianity*, 3rd ed. (Stamford, CT: Cengage Learning, 2015), 203.

3. For a detailed discussion of these issues, see Erwin Lutzer, *The Doctrines That Divide: A Fresh Look at the Historic Doctrines That Separate Christians*, 2nd ed. (Grand Rapids: Kregel, 1998).

4. William Stevenson, *The Story of the Reformation* (Richmond: John Knox, 1959), 84.

Chapter 16 Calvinism's Lasting Influence

1. Timothy George, *Theology of the Reformers* (Nashville: Broadman, 1988), 167.

2. William Stevenson, *The Story of the Reformation* (Richmond: John Knox, 1959), 91–92.

3. Stevenson, *Story of the Reformation*, 92.

4. Sidney Z. Ehler and John B. Morrall, *Church and State through the Centuries: A Collection of Historic Documents with Commentaries* (New York: Biblo and Tannen, 1967), 211.

5. *Occasional Services: A Companion to Lutheran Book of Worship* (Minneapolis: Augsburg, 1982), 18.

Chapter 17 Is the Reformation Over?

1. Mark A. Noll and Carolyn Nystrom, *Is the Reformation Over?* (Grand Rapids: Baker Academic, 2005), 84.

2. Noll and Nystrom, *Is the Reformation Over?*, 84.

3. "Evangelicals and Catholics Together," in *Evangelicals and Catholics Together at Twenty*, ed. Timothy George and Thomas G. Guarino (Grand Rapids: Baker Academic, 2015), 6–23.

4. Noll and Nystrom, *Is the Reformation Over?*, 90–91.

5. Noll and Nystrom, *Is the Reformation Over?*, 109.

6. Scott M. Manetsch, "Is the Reformation Over? John Calvin, Roman Catholicism, and Contemporary Ecumenical Conversations," *Themelios* 36, no. 2 (August 2011), http://themelios.thegospelcoalition.org/article/is-the-reformation-over-john-calvin-roman-catholicism-and-contemporary-ecum.

7. *Catechism of the Catholic Church* (New York: Doubleday, 1995), 275.

8. Ludwig Ott, *Fundamentals of Catholic Dogma* (St. Louis: B. Herder, 1955), 213.

9. St. Alphonsus de Liguori, *The Glories of Mary* (Brooklyn: Redemptorist Fathers, 1931), 160.

10. *Catechism*, 384–85.

11. *Catechism*, 381.

12. *Catechism*, 385.

13. *Catechism*, 411.

14. The book is not available in English. It was reprinted in Italian in 2013, after he became pope.

Image Credits

Map on pages iv–v © Baker Publishing Group. Map by International Mapping.

Image on page xv © *Life of Martin Luther and heroes of the reformation* / H. Breul; original by H. Brückner. Public domain.

Image on page 4 *Abbé pratiquant la simonie*, by Gratianus. Public domain.

Image on page 5 Jensky codex, 1490s. Public domain.

Image on page 9 Lutherdenkmal, Worms, 1868 by Ernst Rietschel. Phograph by Immanuel Giel. Public domain.

Image on page 10 © Universal History Archive/UIG / Bridgeman Images.

Image on page 12 William Frederick Yeames, 1835–1918. Public domain.

Image on page 14 © Papal Bull of Pope Urban VIII / 1637 / Aberystwyth University School of Art Gallery & Museum. Used with permission.

Image on page 18 Spiezer Chronik, 1485. Public domain.

Image on page 23, portrait of Pope Leo X with Two Cardinals by Raphael, circa 1517. Public domain.

Image on page 25 © Galleria degli Uffizi, Florence, Italy / Bridgeman Images.

Image on page 28 © Universal History Archive/UIG / Bridgeman Images.

Image on page 35 portrait of Martin Luther as an Augustinian monk by Lucas Cranach the Elder. Public domain.

Image on page 40 © Alinari / Bridgeman Images.

Image on page 44 Albrecht Dürer, 1496. Public domain.

Image on page 46 © The Stapleton Collection / Bridgeman Images.

Image on page 53 Leipzig Thomaskirche by Dirk Goldhahn. Public domain.

Image on page 58 Marktplatz, Wittenberg, by Johann Gottfried Schadow, 1805. Public domain.

Image on page 74 © Archives Charmet / Bridgeman Images.

Image on page 77 portrait of Charles V on Horseback by Anthony van Dyck, 1620. Galleria degli Uffizi, Florence, Italy. Public domain.

Image on page 78 © Bibliotheque Nationale, Paris, France / Bridgeman Images.

Image on page 82 Luther at the Diet of Worms, by Anton von Werner, 1877. Public domain.

Image on page 92 © Photograph by Jean-Christophe Benoist. Licensed under CC BY 2.5 via Wikimedia Commons.

Image on page 94 © Victoria & Albert Museum, London, UK / Bridgeman Images.

Image on page 97 by Lucas Cranach the Elder, 1537. Public domain.

Image on page 105 Jäcklein Rohrbach Burned Alive, 1551, drawing from Peter Harrer from Description of the Peasants' War. Public domain.

Image on page 110 Desiderius Erasmus, 1622, by Hendrick de Keyser. Public domain.

Image on page 117 © Melinda Cousins. Used with permission.

Image on page 120 by Torsten Schleese. Public domain.

Image on page 127 © Paul T. McCain. 2006. Used with permission. Lutherhaus Museum, Wittenberg, Germany.

Images on page 131 © Sammlungen auf der Wartburg, Eisenach, Germany / Bridgeman Images.

Image on page 134 Private collection of S. Whitehead. Public domain.

Image on page 135 *Luther Making Music in the Circle of His Family*, 1875, by Gustav Spangenberg. Public domain.

Image on page 140 © Paul T. McCain. Licensed under CC BY-SA 2.5 via Wikipedia.

Image on page 143 by Roland Zumbühl. Public domain.

Image on page 150 © The Stapleton Collection / Bridgeman Images.

Top image on page 153 by Heinrich Thomann (1748–1794). Public domain.

Image on page 163 © Yann, 2009. Used with permission.

Image on page 166 © Universal History Archive/UIG / Bridgeman Images.

Image on page 167 Christian Fritzsch (b. 1660) Mittweida, Bautzen, Sachsen, Germany. Public domain.

Image on page 168 © Andy Brinkman. Used with permission.

Image on page 172 © Helena Geri. Used with permission.

Image on page 176 by Francois Dubois (born ca. 1529). Public domain.

Image on page 178 statue of John Knox in New College, Edinburgh / by John Hutchison. Photo © Stephen C. Dickson. Used with permission.

Image on page 182 © Private Collection / Bridgeman Images.

Image on page 184 © De Agostini Picture Library / A. Vergani / Bridgeman Images.